LIVING

MARK'S STORY

GREGORY J. LAUGHERY

Living Mark's Story

© 2017 Gregory J. Laughery

Without limiting the rights under copyright reserved above, no part of this publication may be reproduced, stored in, or introduced into a retrieval system, or transmitted in any form or by any means (electronic, mechanical, photocopying, or otherwise), without the prior written permission from the publisher, except where permitted by law, and except in the case of brief quotations embodied in critical articles and reviews. For information, write: info@destinee.ch

Reasonable care has been taken to trace original sources and copyright holders for any quotations appearing in this book. Should any attribution be found to be incorrect or incomplete, the publisher welcomes written documentation supporting correction for subsequent printing.

Some Scripture quotations are taken from the Holy Bible, New International Version®. NIV®. Copyright ©1973, 1978, 1984 by International Bible Society.
Used by permission of Zondervan. All rights reserved. Other Scripture quotations are taken from New Revised Standard Version of the Bible, copyright © 1989 by the Division of Christian Education of the National Council of the Churches of Christ in the USA. Used by permission. All rights reserved.

Published by Destinée S.A., www.destinee.ch
All rights reserved by the author.

Print ISBN 978-1-938367-35-9

CONTENTS

Introduction 1
Reading Mark's Story 8
   1:1 - 13 17
   1:14 - 45 22
   2:1 - 3:6 27
   3:7 - 35 34
   4:1 – 34 40
   4:35 – 5:43 (1) 44
   4:35 - 5:43 (2) 48
   6:1 – 30 53
   6:30 – 7:23 58
   7:24 – 8:21 62
   8:22 – 9:1 68
   9:1 – 13 72
   9:14 – 50 77
   10:1 – 52 83
   11:1 – 33 89
   12:1 – 44 95
   13:1 – 37 100
   14:1 – 72 104
   15:1 – 47 109
   16:1 - 8 114

INTRODUCTION

One of the salient features of the twenty-first century is that we are living in post-Christian times. Christianity seems to be facing a steady decline—losing its traction, coherence, and credibility. Many of our churches have become corporations run by the principles of consumerism and good marketing skills. Unfortunately, all too often the founding stories of the faith are distorted beyond recognition and used as manipulative tools to maintain the status quo.

In his book *The Incredible Shrinking Church* (2008), Frank Page predicts that half of the thousands of Southern Baptist churches will no longer exist in 2030, and his estimation likely holds true for many other denominations as well. Page cites several reasons for this demise including lower birth rates, changing demographics, and cultures increasingly hostile to the Christian faith. We might add to these an internal disintegration, where our love and unity have been replaced by judgment and estrangement, which in turn raises significant questions concerning the authenticity of Christianity, or perhaps more acutely, why we should even bother to hold onto the present version of it at all.

While these reasons help explain our drift towards the post-Christian, I believe there is another factor that contributes to the decline: we have not handled the biblical text well. There has been a tendency to read it with a *make it up as we go along* methodology. The perversion of the text, to the degree that we can hardly recognize it as a biblical word, has severe consequences when it comes to understanding God, nature, the self, and the other. I'll say more about that in a moment.

In addition to Page's book, there has been a myriad of others recently released concerning the state of the church in the Western world. While coming from different perspectives, they share one thing in common: the church is in trouble. Many people are facing serious questions about the condition and function of the church. The diminishing church in the West today is often front page news. Thus, the previously held mighty notion of 'the church' is inevitably beginning to corrode before our very eyes, and we may query whether it is possibly going to fade from the scene entirely.

To focus briefly on this for a moment, it's no secret that many European churches are being sold off to developers and art galleries. Only a small amount of people attend church in many of the countries of a now-progressive, post-religious Europe. If this decline continues, as some statistics show, church membership could all but disappear in many Western nations.

Considering the United States, there is no question that the country is still under the influence of some big churches; however, the impact of the church on mainstream culture continues its downward spiral towards irrelevance. No doubt there are lots of church buildings – someone recently told me of a Texas church that is undertaking a new $47 million, or something to that extent, building project – and if I can hazard a guess, there will probably be a new bowling alley and health club included, so that believers don't have to mess around with those unbeliever types when indulging in these activities. Often, but not always, this type of situation perpetuates a disembodied Christian faith, which has been gutted and emptied of truth and love. Buildings and programs take precedence over people, and when that happens, we're destined for serious problems.

As mentioned earlier, when referring to Western culture, we are living in "post-Christian" times, and in my estimation, many churches are perpetuating, rather than combatting such a notion. But what does *p-C* mean? Stuart Murray, in his book, *Post-Christian: Church and Mission in a Strange New World*, (2004), defines it this way: "Post-Christian is the culture that emerges as the Christian faith loses coherence within a society that has been definitively shaped by the Christian story, and as the institutions that have been developed to express Christian convictions decline in influence." (6)

Generally speaking, this is a pretty accurate description – therefore, not only do we find ourselves in a post-modern world, but increasingly in a post-Christian one. However, this may not be an altogether negative assessment if we consider that post-Christian is a valid response to what is frequently inauthentic, trite, and superficial, or nearer to pretending, than the real thing.

Most believers, I would argue, would have some serious questions about the trends and rhythms of twentieth and twenty-first century Christianity and its ability to have a credible impact on our lives or Western culture. Might we be living in times when what we have known as church is falling apart? And if so, how are we to find our way towards renewal and hope – something new and living – which can emerge from the meltdown?

One of the factors I touched on earlier that contributes to the decline of faith and that is in desperate need of change is the way we read the biblical story. If the Western church and culture are to begin to recover from the staggering blows they have – by and large – brought upon themselves, it is crucial that the recovery include a diligent study of the biblical text. We could add to this some other factors, including investigating the natural world and embracing Christ as Lord of all of life, but for the moment let's focus on the text.

Reading, studying, and appropriating the truths encoded in the biblical text are essential to Christian existence, as well as to the impact Christians have on the world. However, our approach is often flawed – our reading habits sub-consciously aim to control the text, rather than allow it to bewilder us and infiltrate our lives, which inevitably prevents it from reading us. Stephen Fowl and Greg Jones in their fine book *Reading in Communion*, (1991), make a valid point: "Christian communities must be aware of the possibilities of interpreting Scripture in such a way that it supports rather than subverts corrupt and sinful practices. We need to learn to read the Scriptures over against ourselves rather than simply for ourselves." (41-42)

That is, we tend to form reading habits that presume that we see and hear, when, in reality, we are truly blind and deaf. Take, for example, consumer or pietistic modes of reading. These never challenge our practices and tend to leave our lives intact and unaffected. Such readings mirror cultural or religious pursuits and frequently affirm the status quo, without illuminating any need to change. A wrongly targeted hermeneutics of both trust and suspicion are at work here to silence the text.

Two other modes of reading are widely practiced, but with equally unfortunate results. The first is the "I'm always right" mode. Those who read the biblical text with this perspective often use it as a collection of proof texts, that is, singling-out one text here and another there to prove their interpretation is always the correct one. The text becomes a hammer, and you're the nail who takes a pounding. Usually, this type of reader has already made up their mind about what the text says, before actually reading it carefully.

The second mode is more congenial and perhaps quite attractive to many of us. This is the "I feel it" mode. Those who read Scripture in this mode reduce a passage of Scripture to mean what they feel it means. This mode of reading is similar to the widely misleading statement of the literary critic Stanley Fish: the reader's response is not *to* the meaning, it *is* the meaning.

The "I'm always right" mode attempts to be entirely objective, while the "I feel it" mode aims at pure subjectivity. Neither is plausible. Certainly, there are many other modes of reading, but suffice it to say that those that have been mentioned so far are what I would categorize as *worse* modes of reading the text. Our lives tend to be so loaded with assumptions that force us into monologues, whereas a better mode of reading would develop the space needed for dialogue. Since there are no perfect modes available, we have to aim at crafting a *better* reading strategy.

One of the most important characteristics of a better reading mode is to highlight and understand the context. Read the biblical text in context – there is always a historical, literary, cultural, and theological context that is important to know more about and to seek to understand further. Be well informed here, and you'll be in less danger of misreading.

In addition to context, there are important questions to consider. Who was the narrator/author? Who was the audience? Why was the text written? What would the words used have been likely to mean at the time of writing? What does the text say to us/me in the midst of our contexts? We are not neutral observers and therefore always part of a context, which will invariably have an impact on the reading of the text.

Thinking seriously about applying a mode for a closer reading of the text will help us in our tendencies to over read or under read it to suit our purposes. In so doing, strangely, yet wonderfully we may find that the text can speak and touch our lives, even in astounding ways that ripple out into the world.

Beginning from our cultural context and current understanding, we find that we not only appropriate the text, but need to be read by it, which engages us in redemptive and sometimes formative explanations of God, others, the world, and ourselves, and leads to new and better understandings. Such new understandings begin to awaken us to the living, dynamic, exciting and confronting message of the text, which in turn takes on a latent or even somewhat marginalized faith and moves it towards being more real and authentic.

Re-reading stories of beginnings; Israel, Jesus, the church, helps us rediscover the subversive and radical way in which God has, is, and will reveal the destiny of humanity and the world. God's gracious trajectory of transformation and renewal is to be translated into our lives as we seek to live in the hope that manifests itself in acts of love and justice, which lead us on in the path of the Crucified and Risen One, and more deeply into community with God and each other.

So, the world of the biblical text engages us as a whole person – imagination, reason, senses, experiences, emotions, practices, and bodies. If the church – or let's say, the Christians who fill the seats – are to be known by truth and love, then we have a responsibility to be better informed about what the text says, to the degree that it is true.

One of our goals together throughout this book will be to engage with the text more deeply, which will hopefully allow it to speak in fresh ways, and in so doing, begin to rekindle a legitimate passion for the Christian faith. We do this not only for ourselves, but for a world in desperate need of the good news of the gospel. In the face of living in post-Christian times, the crisis of credibility, and an increasingly skeptical post-trust culture, changes are necessary. In addition to better reading strategies for Mark's story, here are a few more suggestions for how we can contribute to reversing the flow:

> Be living testimonies of God's truth, grace, and love in serving others.
>> Engage nature and people for the sake of Christ.
>> Practice appropriate levels of confidence and humility in apologetics.

Promote credible scholarship in theology, philosophy, science, literature, and other disciplines.
Produce creative and interesting music, poetry, and art.
Be informed about politics, economics,
and social work. Get involved with integrity.

READING MARK'S STORY

To read and hear the gospel of Mark is to enter into a *possible* world; a world of subversive reversals of perspective, intrigue, mystery, and strange riddles, with Jesus as its central protagonist. When we enter this narrative world, we encounter battles between God and Satan, angels and demons, with the fate of humanity hanging in the balance. Far from a simple story, filled with easy answers or a basic list of rules to follow, Mark's story is explosive. Readers are challenged to participate in the recounting and to lose their lives for the sake of Jesus so that they, in turn, may find them. This compelling story is thus presented as a drama to be performed——acted out——lived, in order to cultivate imaginative spirituality and thereby have an impact on the whole person. The world of self-serving power, fame, and control is being shattered, and the embrace of a *possible* world will lead to life after death.

This transforming of worlds takes place as Mark's story orchestrates a series of events and turns them into a symphony. We find there are a multiplicity of tones, notes, and instruments playing together, with an improvisation on the composed score, while still maintaining a single rhythm and theme—the gospel of Jesus Christ.

As we approach this text together, let me say that I would like us to view exploring this gospel as something of an experiment. We'll learn some new vocabulary, seek to read the text as narrative, and find our way through the story as the *narrator* alerts us and directs our path. This is, after all, the narrator's job – whether it is accomplished successfully or not, remains to be seen.

I'll start off with a quote from one of the most widely read books on the gospel of Mark, *Let the Reader Understand* by Robert M. Fowler (1991). Ponder this quote for a few moments:

> "The shift from talking about the gospel per se to talking about the experience of reading the Gospel brings with it a number of shifts. (2) .... a shift away from looking for a static structure in the text and toward an awareness of the dynamic, temporal experience of reading the text." (3)

Now, this part I think is really important:

> "No longer can meaning be understood to be a stable, determinate content that lies buried within a text, awaiting excavation. Rather meaning becomes a dynamic event in which we participate. Furthermore, the shift from meaning-as-content to meaning-as-event leads us to understand the workings of the language of the Gospel in new ways. No longer can the language of the Gospel be regarded as referential or informative. It has become rhetorical, affective, and powerful." (3)

While Fowler has some useful insights, he unhelpfully proposes an either/or polarization. Statements like:

> "No longer can meaning be understood to be a stable, determinate content ... but rather meaning becomes a dynamic event"

indicate that he puts meaning as content on one pole and meaning as event on another. My question is: Why can't we have both? Why do I have to choose whether meaning is a dynamic event or a stable content in this narrative? In other words, perhaps there is a notion of meaning and meaning for me ... or even truth, and truth for me ... and that one need not cancel out the other. If this is the case, polarization would have to be replaced by a dialogue between these two. If we don't have a dialogue, it seems to me that we embrace polarizations, which in this kind of context are going to be problematic because they force us in false directions where we risk losing the direction of the story.

As we go through this story, try to remember: why not both? Do I really have to choose between one or the other, in the way that Fowler has suggested? I would say no. I don't think that we do. I would go for a "both/and" ... in this context, rather than an "either/or."

Hopefully, this gives you a brief snapshot of one influential type of discussion that pertains to reading the gospel of Mark. Do we need to be concerned about authors anymore? Do we need to be concerned about meaning as a stable content in the text? Is meaning just a dynamic event for me? Should meaning solely be something for me to participate in? So again, maybe both narrators and readers are important for a better understanding of this story.

If you would like to, open the biblical text to the gospel of Mark and read chapters 1 to 3:6. This is the first segment in the sequence of the unfolding story. The narrator is telling the story and will introduce several key characters here and there as we go along, notably Jesus, God, the Pharisees, and someone with an unclean spirit.

I encourage you to photocopy the story and then mark it up so that you have the narrator's words, and the characters words, as well as the plot trajectory for the storyline. Better connecting to these literary features of the story will have a powerful effect on the reading of Mark's gospel.

It is all too easy for us to just read through a text lackadaisically, and if you photocopy it, then you can do what you want. You can underline things, you can put question marks, and you can write comments. One method I find helpful is highlighting all that the characters have to say. This sets them apart in a way that reading might not. To become more attuned to what the characters are saying, how the narrator is setting up these roles, and so forth, heightens the intrigue and therefore might be a worthwhile endeavor.

Today, more than ever, biblical interpreters are drawing upon the knowledge of the history, societies, cultures, and texts of ancient times to understand the biblical text better. One of the most prominent features of this has been the rediscovery of the importance of narrative. No doubt this has something to do with the dramatic rise of our own culture's attraction to literature and especially the significantly renewed interest in stories and tales. Think of the fascination, for better or worse, with *The Lord of the Rings*, *Harry Potter*, and *The Chronicles of Narnia* – or with the music of Rhapsody and others who are telling stories through their musical compositions.

Yet, the biblical writers were way ahead of us. Literature and stories – narratives – were highly important in their time as they wrote complex and careful recountings of what God was thought to be accomplishing with and through the created world, humanity, Israel, and Jesus Christ. The biblical text is a mega-story recounted through different literary forms and styles and the task before us is to attempt to follow the story of Mark's gospel.

Let's begin by noting a few things—I've used the words *narrative* and *narrator* numerous times. It would be helpful to discover what they have to do with the biblical text. In 1981 Robert Alter published a book entitled *The Art of Biblical Narrative*, and narrative criticism was born. As narrative, narrator, and narrative criticism are fairly recent developments in the study of biblical literature; it's important to underline that some definitions are still in the formation process. Nevertheless, I want to give you something to go on, so with what we have available to us, let's try to expand our horizons.

To better hear, read, and live the story of Mark's gospel it is important to know this: The narrator, the voice of the recounter, is the one who tells the story. Often, though not always in biblical accounts, the narrator is hidden behind the story. Yet, all narratives have a narrative strategy, and we will hear the voice of the narrator as we discover how the story unfolds.

In Mark the storyteller is an "omniscient" narrator — one who can be inside people, know their thoughts and feelings, take part in private scenes with one or more characters when not present, and even be in two places simultaneously. As readers of the story we usually assume the trustworthiness of the narrator who is telling it – we stick to the storyline – or we stop reading.

How about narrative? What is narrative? Umberto Eco, of *The Name of the Rose* fame, suggests that to tell a story or write a narrative you have to construct a world. From this perspective we could say, Mark's gospel is not merely information, but a created story world – *both related to and distinct from the real world.* I'll say more about that later.

Eco's suggestion, while helpful, needs to be supplemented by another feature of story. Stories connect actions – narrative creates causal relations between one action and another. Think about this: "she sees a cow in the field" is not a narrative – "she sees a cow in the field and milks it" is.

One last feature of narrative to be mentioned, brought to light by Paul Ricoeur, is time. What is recounted in narrative takes place in time and makes time. Stories have a temporal dimension that is not to be missed or ignored if we are to understand them better. But surely there are at least a few other important elements of narrative: plot, the point of view, characters, intrigue, suspense, drama, audience-reader... the list goes on.

Now, let's consider narrative criticism: it is, by definition, the study of reading a story – its effects, its identity, its arrangement, and its strategy aimed at the reader. Narrative criticism is a more holistic approach concerned with plot, characters, and conflicts as they fit together as a whole – and not merely with what occurred. A strong emphasis on unity is perhaps the most salient feature of narrative criticism. The gospel of Mark as a coherent and unified story tells about the Kingdom of God, Jesus, sin, faith, possession-dispossession, human transformation and much more.

Like a portrait painting exists as related and distinct to its model, so the gospel of Mark is related and distinct to what it is portraying. Mark is not a direct representation of events in Jesus' life and times – it is a creatively constructed story that has a world of its own. Having some knowledge of historical events is crucial for understanding Mark, but it is not one and the same with using Mark to reconstruct these events. On the subject of history and the biblical text let me say this: there is a fascinating and important discussion going on here (see Paul Ricoeur's work).

Ricoeur has entered this debate with a number of articles on biblical interpretation and the question of history, which are also addressed in his three-volume work *Time and Narrative*. But, what is history? This seems an easy enough to question to answer until someone raises it. Ricoeur's notion is that there are three types of historiography or written accounts of events in time. Let's explore these.

First, the documentary – this seeks to establish the verifiable facts – what battle was won, when, and by whom, for example. Second, is the explicative – this attempts to weigh up an event from social, economic, or political angle – in other words, what resulted from the battle? Third, is the poetic, which rewrites and organizes the past into a sequence of stories through which a community of readers learns about itself – this work of interpreting draws out a conclusion as to why the battle was won. Poetic history, according to Ricoeur, cannot be forced into the same true/false options as documentary history. Its truth, Ricoeur suggests, is in the interpretation of the past and the manner in which it illumines the present for a community of readers.

If we take this threefold portrayal seriously, we conclude that there is not just one way in which history is written, but several. If the gospel of Mark is historical, it would seem rather important to seek to discover its historiographical purposes. I think we will do well to keep the notion of the *poetic* in mind. However, it's important to understand that Mark's story cannot be reduced to any one pure type of historiography. His narrative leans in the direction of poetic historiography—the narrator is continually interpreting and pointing toward the significance of Jesus' manifestations of power – teaching, healing, and exorcism, to name just three.

I would like to conclude this introduction by giving you a few readerly directions concerning the gospel of Mark. Several key markers will guide us on our journey; the narrator does everything possible to assist readers in understanding the meaning of the text and in recognizing the significance of living out that meaning as followers of the Crucified and Risen One.

One of the most remarkable traits in Mark's gospel story is urgency – this is connected to Jesus' pronouncement in 1:15 when he says 'the time is fulfilled.' The narrator uses – immediately, at once, quickly, over forty times. In chapter 1 alone we find this feature in: 1:12, 18, 20, 21, 23, 28, 29, and 30. The narrative moves at breakneck speed – little development and always rushing into the next scene. Urgency marks time – another dimension of time is days, not months or years – the narrator uses this chronological configuration to heighten the imminence of what is taking place. The last feature of time is the framing of beginning (1:1) and end (13:13) – the narrator wants to show readers that time is not indefinite and that there is an urgency before the end to decide and act upon who Jesus is in light of the arrival of the KOG. This world of time, for the narrator, is a battleground between good and evil, God and Satan, humans and demons, Jesus and the religious authorities, and Jesus and the disciples. In such a world, time is crucial and salvific – time is 'now' time – and people need to be vigorously awakened to the tremendous significance of God's saving actions, make a decision about following Jesus, and live a radically changed and transformed life.

Another feature that marks this gospel is conflict. We'll find the narrator often presents Jesus encountering conflict in a number of different scenarios: with Satan in 1:13, unclean spirits in 1:24, teachers of the law in 2:7, Pharisees in 2:24, family in 3:20-35, nature in 4:48, demons in 5:15, and disciples in 8:14-21. What is important for us to understand here is the origin, climax, increase or diminishment, and resolution (or lack thereof) in these conflict contexts as well as what they tell us about Jesus and those who oppose him and the KOG.

One further feature to touch on is interpolation. Our narrator repeatedly inserts one story within another to enhance meaning and create an echo effect that reverberates through the narrative. There are many examples: 3:20-35 (22-30), 4:1-20 (10-13), 5:21-43 (25-34) and so on throughout the story. It seems likely that the narrator uses this narrative strategy of two interpolated scenes, so the reader can see how they interpret each other. Let's briefly look at chapter 3:20-35.

We may query whether it is an accident that the narrator brings in Jesus' family (just after appointing the *twelve* in the previous scene), whom readers have heard nothing about until now. The interpolated story in verses 22-30 is a response to Jesus' family who seriously believes he may be out of his mind. In fact, after the teachers of the law accuse him of being possessed by Beelzebul, the prince of demons, Jesus, with sound poise, refutes them eloquently and intelligibly.

Now notice the arrival of the family, in verse 31– the narrator plays on plays off this – they are *outside* twice far from Jesus, while others are *inside* twice close to Jesus. Thus, he is portrayed as the forerunner of a new family of the people of God who is connected not by flesh and blood, but by doing the will of God. I'll say more about this later.

Permit me to point out a final feature — the narrator frequently surprises readers by reversing roles. Those who think they see and hear are blind and deaf, while those who are blind and deaf see and hear. Thus, a life of following Jesus is not about possessing people and things, but about dispossession, being willing to let go, to take risks, to be courageous and not fear – to break – rather than embrace oppressive cultural practices. It is to be de-powered from a lack of faith to be empowered to faith in God – to be great you have to be least; the first will be last and the last first. Those who want to save their lives will have to lose them for the sake of Jesus and the gospel. Perhaps, the most striking reversal of all is that the unclean spirits and demons recognize Jesus immediately, while the disciples obliviously fail to perceive who he is time and time again.

Being aware of these structural features of the gospel of Mark – time, conflict, interpolation, and role reversal – help us to understand the story better. Time, including especially salvific time, is urgent – follow Jesus: hear, read, and perform the good news of the KOG. Will we be in conflict with Jesus or will we seek to identify ourselves with him? What's at risk? Is Jesus out of his mind? Is he demon possessed? This inaugurator of a new family and world has arrived with a mission rooted in the values of God's rule in the face of accusation, opposition, and eventually, death. And finally, in consideration of role reversal, which role will you play in the story?

1:1 - 13

The first thirteen verses of the narrative are the prologue. This introductory, yet highly significant material, gives the narrator an opportunity to prepare and enlighten readers, before recounting the actions and activities of Jesus Christ, which begin in verse 14. Observant readers of the story need to be aware of this important front-loaded matter to have a fuller picture of what God is 'now' doing. It is crucial to remember before we get into the story, that the prologue provides readers with essential insights into Mark's narration, which characters in the story are not privileged to have. As enlightening as the prologue is, the narrator continues to raise questions concerning the reader's world and perspective, rather than providing easy answers that require little thought, conviction, or participation.

The Markan prologue opens with these intriguing words: "The beginning of the gospel of Jesus Christ." The narrator wants readers to know that something is about to occur that hasn't previously taken place. This story of Jesus Christ, his identity, mission, and revelation will point us in an uncharted direction. The aim here is to alert readers that something completely new is going to happen. Neither Matthew nor Luke referred to their writings as 'gospel.' Consequently, the narrator of Mark is likely to be embarking on an innovative literary adventure, which may nevertheless fit loosely into the context of a Jewish/Greco-Roman biography.

So, exactly, what is new? The genitive construction, 'gospel of Jesus Christ' immediately raises a query. Should readers understand this to suggest that Jesus Christ is this gospel *or* merely a proclaimer of it? At the onset of the prologue, it seems likely that there is a fair amount of purposeful vagueness that encourages readers not to choose – Jesus Christ is *both* proclaimer *and* content of this gospel. We should not always assume that the use of ambiguity in biblical stories is negative, as it may, in fact, enhance meaning rather than detract from it. What is important to realize is this: intentional ambiguity of this sort will aid readers in envisioning truths within the tension of a both-and scenario – Jesus Christ is *both* proclaimer *and* content of the gospel, rather than either one or the other.

But if this is the case, it should raise another question: What is the gospel – this good news? One of the features of the good news in the prologue is simply Jesus' arrival as Messiah - it is he who was prophesied to create a new exodus, liberate Israel from exile, and establish the KOG in a world dominated by the forces and powers of evil. To confirm the newness of God's purpose and intent for this good news the narrator moves readers backward from the prologue, reversing the flow. Amidst the impending drama of this story, there has been an underlying assurance that a new age would arrive – the expected, long-awaited era – when one would come to mark out the fulfillment of these promises. Finally, the time had come for the Lord to liberate his people once again.

The narrator selects well known OT texts that are a key to the gospel's arrival—a conflation of Malachi 3:1, Exodus 23:20, and Isaiah 40:3, which appear under the heading: "As it has been written in Isaiah." The mention of Isaiah highlights the aim of the narrator to underscore the prophetic character of these three lines now converging in time. Let me explain.

The first line *streams* from the life of Israel's Exodus and the direction received during periods of wandering in the wilderness/desert. The second line *foretells* the coming of the one who will *judge* Israel for its sinful ways. And the third line *emphasizes*, at the point of Israel's liberation from exile that God would indeed come to release his people. This streaming, foretelling, and emphasizing are configured in this potent manner to suggest that a new exodus as the shattering of Israel's exile, is now at hand. The uploading of this picture contributes to the development of what is to follow in the prologue, but it also is of considerable importance for the unfolding story of the gospel of Jesus Christ. The next picture portrayed in the prologue for the reader is the actual coming of John in the wilderness/desert. His role is messenger and voice to prepare the way.

Just as quickly as the narrator moved us back in God's story, we are now again moving forward with the entrance of John, the messenger, in the wilderness. John is baptizing and proclaiming to the Jewish people that through repentance they shall be released from sin in the light of the gospel. This *is* the time. John's location is shockingly removed from ordinary daily life—he's essentially in the wilderness/desert, separate from others as well as Jerusalem and its ideologies. This was truly a sign of hope and fulfillment to all who came. Repentance without sacrifice in Israel was, in this cultural context, bordering on blasphemous. Apparently, John's message – "repent" – stirred up a fair amount of intrigue and interest. Jews flowed out into the wilderness, confessed, and were baptized.

A further point of interest - and no doubt important to the narrator - was to recount to readers John's appearance and diet. These traits confirm and highlight John's prophetic role and may even further underline his Elijah connections in light of the proclamation he is professing. John affirms that the one coming after him has a strength and worth far greater than his own. His baptism was a water rite, but the coming one – the stronger one – will saturate Israel with the Holy Spirit. The movement here appears to be from ceremonial washing, which even John indicates is not sufficient, to the creation of a new people of God in light of the fulfillment of the coming One, who will inaugurate the new exodus in the KOG.

The prologue continues in verses 9-11 with Jesus' arrival on the scene. The narrator indicates that Jesus comes out of Nazareth in Galilee to be baptized by John 'in those days,' a highly Semitic manner of speech—this signifies that this is something and someone altogether new and unique. Ironically, in contrast to the Jewish crowds flowing out of Jerusalem and Judea, Jesus arrives from Galilee. The coming One paradoxically enters the prologue by way of a water baptism by John—this highlights Jesus' alignment with the people of God and the transfer, for the reader, from one trajectory in the OT toward God's all-encompassing purpose with Jesus. After his baptism reception, the One – Jesus – has a vision of a tear in heaven, no doubt reminiscent for the narrator of many OT pictures that portray God opening heaven to descend and abide with his people. The drama of tearing open heaven is a powerful way of revealing that something surprising is about to take place. Just then Jesus sees the Spirit descending to or upon him, which from the narrative perspective, is a confirmation of the fulfillment of the times as Jesus is more and more clearly identified as the long-awaited Messiah of God. There does not seem to be any particular hidden significance as to why the narrator uses the imagery of a dove. At the time, doves didn't carry any symbolic or theological overtones—so it is probably best to interpret this as Jesus perceiving the invisible Spirit in the visible form of a dove, which signifies that he is indeed the Christ.

But the narrative doesn't stop there—it appears that we have a second confirmation. Previously, there was a voice calling in the wilderness/desert, this time it is a voice from heaven foretelling the coming of hope and fulfillment. God is speaking from outside places that go beyond the norm of everyday life. A voice from heaven and wilderness/desert voices alike need to be heard, as we move further into the narrative world, which in a startling and outrageous way begins to transform and change our own.

God's voiced proclamation assures readers that Jesus is the real thing - the beloved authentic Son - promised from the times of the OT in whom God is now pleased. These OT images (Isaiah 42:1-4 and Psalm 2:7) give readers a striking portrayal of Jesus as the unique son of God who will carry forward God's promise of a Messiah-servant-being who would bring forth the long-awaited KOG. After this verbal confirmation from God, the Spirit instantly drives Jesus away from one wilderness and into another – to a place outside, further away from daily life, everyday contexts, and the flow of crowds flocking to John.

Notice Jesus is portrayed as entirely passive in the narrator's recounting, while the angels and the Spirit are active. The narrator offers readers an inside perspective beyond the norms of human affairs to showcase the Spirit's role in Jesus' mission of facing conflict, and a power battle that is not entirely played out in daily life situations. Intriguingly, the vivid and striking verb—drive out—for the Spirit's action is used many times in this narrative, most often as we shall see later when Jesus drives out demons. This verb usually connotes motions of conservation or resistance, but the narrator chooses to avoid any such overt suggestions. What is portrayed more clearly is that the authentic, unique Son of God faces this time of conflict through the initiative of the Spirit.

Whatever testing Jesus endures in this outside place, its impact, concerning the unfolding mission of God in these new times, is monumental. Jesus again receives confirmation as God's authentic Son. The protagonist Satan, the adversary, tempts Jesus in the wilderness for a time; this is reminiscent of the previous period of Israel's testing in the outside places—the era in the wilderness before entering the Promised Land. The narrator makes very little of this encounter and the testing connected to it. No sense of victory or defeat – winner or loser. The mention of wild animals may reinforce the picture of an outside place and Israel's wanderings in the wilderness, where God's people are protected from vicious animals; much like Jesus may have now been through the aid of angels. The focus here seems to heighten the drama as the baptized and eventual baptizing Son of God – the coming One – is thrust into conflict in a hostile and threatening environment that is, however, unable to halt God's unfolding mission to Israel and the world through his Son.

With the prologue now set in place, the narrator can, having given readers privileged and crucial information that none of the characters in the story have, now move into recounting more of who Jesus is and what he does as proclaimer and central actor in the narrative. Announcing, inaugurating, and participating in the times of the unfolding KOG will eventually cost Jesus his life – but there is much to explore in and to learn from the story before we get there.

1:14 - 45

As the story proper begins, the narrator will shed greater light on Jesus' mission and identity. Concerned to bring the reader into story time, there is no development of John's arrest at this point, simply because he is no longer on the scene. Forging ahead quickly, the narrator highlights that Jesus takes on the role of the central character and this will underscore both contrast and continuity with the Baptist.

In contrast to John (remember he was outside daily life and everyday matters), Jesus will associate with others in their day to day affairs. Reversing the flow, he will go to the people in towns, villages, and cities proclaiming the good news about God, which he is both bringing and embodying. In continuity with John, Jesus is both proclaiming and calling people to repent. For the first time in the story, he now speaks - Jesus suggests, in a narrative liaison with the prologue, that the fulfillment of prophetic pronouncements have come to fruition - the time has come - something new in the light of the old has arrived. Jesus expresses this by claiming that the KOG has come near - this "coming near" is an indication of timing, the KOG has now drawn nearer humanity in a new way.

The subject of the KOG has been much discussed in books and commentaries. Let's just think of it as *God's rule* and all that this potentially implies. To do so is to make room for the polyphonic character of the term, rather than reducing it to a single referent or meaning. Jesus' statement is saturated with the notion that God is fulfilling the promise that his long-awaited rule is now present, yet still awaits completion. Another helpful way to envision the KOG is as a symbol in tension – past, present, future – already and not yet – arrived and not complete. It aims to arouse a whole constellation of thoughts, feelings, observations, and imaginary processes associated with God ruling in word, deed, and action. A fair bit of the story we hear in Mark's gospel is an expression of this symbol in tension, as it cuts a pathway through a thicket of conflicts, reversals, and antagonisms connected to Jesus' actions and his teaching.

The following words of Jesus – *repent and believe the good news* emphasize two things: first the need to change our ways, reverse our direction; and second, to trust in and be committed to the good news, as it will now unfold in the story from here on out. While readers may be expecting some cataclysmic event, as the KOG has come near, the story of Jesus in Galilee, takes a surprising turn. God's rule is going to manifest itself in some unexpected ways that may surprise us.

The first things connect to the daily activities of walking and fishing. The province of Galilee, in contrast to the small confines of Nazareth, will be the setting of much of the story up to chapter 8. This location provides a Jewish audience, which would have some link with the proclamation of the KOG. Then seeing Simon and Andrew fishing, Jesus invites them to come along – to follow behind him, to become fishers of men and women. Immediately they follow. Two others, the sons of Zebedee, are also called by Jesus and follow him at once. These first disciples will form a core in a group of people through whom aspects of God's rule will eventually become manifest. The quick rhythm of discipleship calling may indicate a previous awareness of - or even encounter with - Jesus, but the narrator gives us little to go on, in order perhaps, to highlight the persuasive authority of the coming One.

The scene, with Jesus and the disciples, now shifts to Capernaum, Sabbath, and the synagogue. Jesus, likely well-known among synagogue leaders, which most Jewish first century readers would easily assume, is teaching in the synagogue. Jesus' teaching astounds the people, who acknowledge his authority over that of their current theological influences. At this very moment, during the normalcy of daily life in a synagogue context, a man possessed by an unclean, evil spirit yells two questions and an exclamation: "What have we to do with you, Jesus of Nazareth? Have you come to destroy us? I know who you are – the Holy One of God." The opposition is announced directly – the unclean spirit assumes that Jesus' presence implies he has a mission of destroying such spirits and reveals what readers – but not yet characters in the story – already know: Jesus is indeed the Holy One of God.

Now with power that will manifest itself in the story several times from here on out, Jesus exorcises this unclean spirit with a command that both silences the spirit and brings it under his control. Jesus' order is obeyed, and the spirit is immediately ripped out of the man with screaming and convulsions. It appears, at least from the narrator's point of view, that Jesus aims to silence the unclean spirit, not destroy it. Again, in response to such a manifestation, the people are astonished. Jesus' power over unclean-evil spirits is remarkable—as readers, we are privy to the knowledge that this is a demonstration of who Jesus is in the context of the arriving KOG.

It is important to note that there were many rumors of exorcists and exorcisms in Jesus' times, but little evidence of their integrity. The credibility and reality of Jesus' exorcism, therefore, creates quite a stir. The amazement of the witnesses at the synagogue provokes much exclamation and excitement surrounding the event. This new teaching is not only authoritative, but the teacher, Jesus, has power beyond anything beheld before. This powerful manifestation of the KOG begins to make Jesus well known in Galilee. Thus the public persona of Jesus now begins to increase and spread like fire in a dry forest.

The story moves ahead quickly, but the scene changes from that of the public sphere to a private one, centering on the disciples. Notice that the next event takes place on the same day, and is a further expression of Jesus' power—first, he heals Simon's mother-in-law without a word, merely through touch. Then, at evening time, returning to the public sphere and keeping with Sabbath regulations, he attends to the public's ailments and exorcism needs. While Jesus is primarily neither healer nor exorcist, the narrator highlights these powerful manifestations to show that Jesus cared for those in need and that his power was indeed superior to any other.

The narrator again, but this time more strongly than Jesus did in verse 25, conveys to readers that Jesus not only drives out demons, but orders them to silence, prohibiting them from publicly proclaiming who he is, at least on the narrative level of the unfolding story. Of course, the narrator makes it clear that readers – not to mention the unclean spirits and demons – know more than the other bystanders in the story who will learn more as the story progresses.

The narrator dramatically opens the next day in darkness, portraying Jesus retreating to a quiet place outside to pray. Most likely aware of this ritual, Simon – perhaps developing into a leader from a narrative standpoint – and the other disciples, are concerned that Jesus could be utilizing his time in a better more productive way back inside the daily life of Capernaum. People were seeking Jesus out, yet he now seems to have other, more private concerns. We begin to experience on the story level a directional division in which the disciples view matters one way, and Jesus, another.

Jesus' response to their critique is explicit: He wants to shift into another phase of activity, travel to other towns and villages, and proclaim the message that the KOG was near. The narrator summarizes in 1:39 that Jesus' directional shift took place. He traveled throughout Galilee proclaiming the good news of his mission, and in the narrator's understanding, continues manifesting his power through demon exorcisms.

In his travels, Jesus receives a man with skin disease, a condition rendering him not only physically, but spiritually unclean (1:40-45). No doubt such people were *outside*, removed to places away from people and normal daily activities. Despite the cultural mandate of exclusion for uncleanliness, this man urgently begs Jesus to take notice, and ultimately, to cleanse him. This interaction indicates that rumors about Jesus were rampant, reaching even to the remote places and disconnected people.

The narrator first explains Jesus' reaction – he was moved deeply by this man; his circumstances, social situation, and degraded condition provoked an emotional response. Jesus then acts – he touches the man and courageously pronounces "I am willing – Be clean." To touch this man was not only to ignore laws of ritual purity, but also risking contamination by the sickness. However, neither prevents Jesus from granting this man's request and at once he is cleansed. Intriguingly, Jesus then forcefully excuses the man saying in verse 44: "see that you say nothing to anyone, but go, show yourself to the priest and offer for your cleansing what Moses commanded, for a proof to them." We discover in the next verse that the man does exactly the opposite, making it difficult for Jesus to enter the town openly.

Perhaps, considering Jesus' words in this verse, this man had intended to disregard Jesus and to pay no attention to the necessary legislation that would confirm his cleanliness. Jesus scolds the cleansed man – he is not to say anything about his cleansing. Ironically, he is instructed to obey ritual legislation, show the priest his healing, and offer sacrifices. Jesus' concern here seems to be for the man, not for the law per se. He knows that following these legal obligations will be the only way that this man can move from the outside and into the rhythm of daily, normal life. The needed testimony to the priestly orders is the offering of sacrifices in combination with the evidence of the cleansed man himself. Jesus is conscious of the amount of controversy this will create concerning his mission and the inauguration of a salvific power that goes far beyond legislation. Given the narrator's next comment, we can't be sure if the man goes into Jerusalem, the only place to offer sacrifices, or if he indeed shows himself to a priest.

What is clear is that the cleansed man disobeyed the first command of Jesus – "see that you say nothing to anyone... ." The unfortunate effect of this, as Jesus seems well aware, is that it begins to have a negative impact on the Galilean mission. The picture we're left with at the end of chapter 1 is that Jesus is now forced to an outside place and away from the life of towns and communities. The misunderstanding crowds and the growing opposition of the authorities are complicating matters and conflict therein increased. Jesus' identity and purpose are in jeopardy. However, as previously seen with John the Baptist, many people are approaching him in the outside places far from everyday life. Outsiders continue to show the way inside, although not always with a conscious recognition of the in-breaking KOG, or he who was inaugurating it.

2:1 - 3:6

In the next part of the story, beginning in 2:1, we read that Jesus becomes embroiled in a number of *conflicts* and *controversies*. The aim of the narrator, at this stage, is to give readers a deeper glimpse into the identity of the Messiah, how his actions manifest the arrival of God's kingdom, and why these dimensions of his person and mission create clashes that will inevitably threaten his life.

So far we have read that Jesus is God's son with whom he is pleased. We have seen Jesus proclaiming the gospel of the coming KOG and extending the invitation to follow him. As readers, and narrative insiders, we know him as a teacher, healer, and exorciser of demons.

Returning to the story following the specific healing of the man with a skin disease in 1:40-45, we recall the result of this cleansing – and ultimately the man's inability to be silent – is that Jesus can no longer openly enter towns as the news about him was spreading. He is forced outside of daily life, away from people, yet in spite of this, they come to him. After Jesus' strong warning to the healed man to keep quiet and to show the priest, offer sacrifices, and be credited as clean is ignored, the narrator prepares us for the rising conflicts that will invariably ensue.

Sometime later, Jesus returns from the outside places to Capernaum, seemingly without detection. Much of the excitement about his teaching and manifestations of power may have subsided in the outside places, and it is time to re-ignite the mission in Capernaum. Interest in Jesus again flourished. He was rumored to be in the house of Simon and Andrew – we might imagine a one-room chalet situated on a small road with a horde of people crowding into a three to five-meter space, and more outside cluttering around the door and flowing out into the narrow street. With this image in mind, picture Jesus speaking to the crowd, proclaiming that the good news of the KOG was finally near – the time of God's rule had arrived in a radically new way.

Just then, arriving on the scene are a group of men carrying a paralytic on a mat. The crowd makes it difficult for the group to get through and bring this person to Jesus. As archaeological excavations of Capernaum reveal, many houses had outside stairs leading up to flat roofs. These men, seemingly, removed the roof (imagine again that small, crowded chalet and the commotion of people on the roof taking off tiles to be able to lower someone down to Jesus). They dug through the thatched mud sealed roofing. Who knows what Jesus and the crowd thought of all this, much less the owner? Were they looking up wondering whether the roof would cave in, or had Jesus just continued speaking? Such curious details are of no interest to the narrator. What takes place next sheds light on why this roof-story is included at this point in the narrative.

From the narrator's perspective, when Jesus sees their faith, as evidenced by their persistence of removing the roof, he ceases to address the crowd and turns to these men. News of Jesus' healing power had preceded him – these people had faith that he would heal again. Jesus' pronouncement – "child, your sins are forgiven," may seem slightly or even awfully strange to us. Original hearers, no doubt, would have been less perplexed. In both the OT and NT contexts, physical healing was sometimes connected to the forgiveness of sin. However, this is not always the case throughout biblical literature. The forgiveness proclaimed by Jesus raised issues for the scribes, stationed nearby, who quietly questioned his motives in performing such an act.

The questions posed here are probably to be understood as a silent accusation of blasphemy. To claim to forgive or to grant forgiveness on God's behalf would have carried the charge of desecrating the oneness of YHWH. Who does Jesus think he is?

At once, Jesus knew the scribes' silent thoughts. The narrator wants readers to know that remarkable power is displayed not only in healing, exorcism, and proclamation, but also in discerning the hearts and minds of the skeptical religious authority. In response to their thoughts, Jesus conversely raises questions publicly, for all to hear. No doubt the silent scribes would have been startled by Jesus reading their minds – How does he know? They may have wondered.

Jesus points out that if the more difficult is accomplished, then the easier would naturally follow. In this context, the easier would be to say "your sins are forgiven," than the excessively more complicated statement to the paralytic – rise and walk. Jesus is willing to act in correlation with his words in order to quell the skepticism he detects in the scribes. Christians, those of us who follow in the footsteps of Jesus, might seriously consider attempting to do the same. As we dialogue with skeptics, let's remember the important connection between what we say and do.

Jesus, in this context, wants them to know that he – self-referenced as Son of Man and notably connected to the Daniel 7 figure who is given authority over humanity – has the power to forgive sins. This manifestation of power and the Son of Man self-identification attached to it would have left the teachers of the law breathless.

Then, Jesus' words, in the story, bring about instant results – the lame man stood, took his mat, and walks for all to see. Jesus shows that he has healed and forgiven sin simultaneously – indeed, the KOG has come near. Nothing could have been more shocking and entirely unprecedented. Everyone was amazed and gave glory to God.

Moving on quickly with that prevalent sense of urgency in Mark's gospel, the next scene is situated near a lake where we find Jesus teaching a crowd of people. Plenty of room here compared to the previous scene. It is good to remember that the last time Jesus was in a "by the lake" vicinity, he called for others to follow him.

He encounters Levi sitting at a tax booth, perhaps in the area performing border duties – a sort of customs official who keeps an eye on various goods that are transported in or out of the region. What better location than by the lake? We can only assume these details since again the narrator doesn't give us all the information. It seems plausible, however, that Jesus had some previous contact or influence on the tax man. At any rate, Levi is told by Jesus, "follow me," and he immediately obliges.

In the next scene, dinner is being served at Levi's house, and Jesus is eating with tax collectors, sinners, and disciples alike. His followers, the narrator informs us, were many. Jesus' popularity is growing, but controversy and conflict lurk nearby, in the suspicions of the threatening religious leaders.

So, here's Jesus in the middle of some dubious characters. Nothing could be worse than a mischievous and dishonest Jewish tax collector who overcharges people while also working for what was considered puppet government authorities. As for sinners, these folks had no particular concern for scribal performances and rituals practiced by Pharisees – they were considered unclean. Think of the tax collectors and sinners as outcasts – they were grouped with the social dregs who failed to measure up to traditional Jewish standards. It's evident that Jesus not only identifies with these outcasts, but in the perspective of the religious authorities, is one himself.

The scribal Pharisees, those within the group who were especially concerned with enforcing a pristine obedience to the law, are outraged by Jesus' behavior on a social, moral, and ritual level. They ask a question, not so much an honest query, but more likely a condemning accusation. Although the question is directed to disciples, Jesus may have been within earshot, or it was passed on to him.

This scribal group, no doubt disturbed by Jesus' actions, openly voices concern – Does he eat with tax collectors and sinners? Jesus reply is two-fold, with one concern: those in need. Doctors don't spend their time nurturing healthy people, but have a responsibility to care for the sick. In the same way, he has come to call sinners into the KOG – not the assumed righteous who already saw themselves as part of it. Jesus is breaking down status quo perspectives, calling for a reinterpretation of cultural and religious understandings.

The third incident in this series of controversy and conflict connects to fasting. It is likely that the narrator positioned this story here to immediately follow the scene with Jesus sharing a meal with outcasts. Notice this time, however, the question is put forward by "some people," who had evidently observed a difference in Jesus' disciples, those of John the Baptist, and the Pharisees.

It's likely that fasting required rather rigorous and regular requirements – ordinances that Jesus' disciples are openly neglecting. These people voice their concern: why aren't Jesus' disciples likewise following the rules and regulations of fasting?

Far from dismissing fasting altogether, as verse 20 indicates, Jesus responds with a question concerning timing. Now is the time is for celebration and festivity, not fasting – the bridegroom is still present with the wedding guests. A wedding not only recognizes, but rejoices in the reality of newness and abundant life. In this context, Jesus' self-reference is both vivid yet veiled – his identity as the bridegroom means that his disciples, during this celebratory time, should not be fasting. Jesus hints in verse 19b that this time of festivity and celebration will not go on indefinitely, and then more emphatically pronounces that when he, the bridegroom, is taken is from them, the time for fasting will resume.

The newness that a wedding brings forth is further illustrated by two short sayings concerning new and old. What Jesus calls *new* is his message of the arrival of the KOG. He deems *old* the traditional ways of being, seeing, and doing that don't embody the uniqueness of the presence of the bridegroom and his manifestation of God's kingship. God is doing something so radically new that it cannot be perpetuated nor restricted by old garments or wineskins.

Up to this point, we have discovered Jesus' new foundational perspectives on forgiveness and release from sin. The last two scenes, concluding this first major segment of the narrative, center on the Sabbath. These scenes introduce the Pharisees for the first time – these religious leaders have serious concerns about the actions of Jesus' disciples who are reportedly doing some form of reaping on the Sabbath.

Their objection and question to Jesus revolve around the legality of what the disciples are doing according to Jewish Sabbath law. What does Jesus have to say concerning this matter?

He offers an example from the OT, Samuel 21:1-6, but his logic in doing so is not readily apparent. The OT scene and the Pharisee's protest seem to have very little in common. These incidents, David's and the one at hand, may have both taken place on the Sabbath, but that's chiefly where the similarities end, save for one important feature. Jesus drives home the point that the key isn't *what* was done on the Sabbath, but *who* was doing it. David surpasses the law and not only does the OT mention this, but it appears to sanction it. Two points: Jesus is greater than David, and the illegality of the disciples' actions are conventional, not as in David's case, formal. On both registers, Jesus is expressing his authority. If what David and his followers did on the Sabbath was accepted, then it follows that the Pharisees have no reason to object to what the disciples of Jesus are doing. Here's why – the Sabbath is made for people, not the other way around. Therefore, it exists to promote blessing, not legalism; rejoicing, not guilt.

Jesus' "Son of Man" statement closes the scene. He allows his disciples to do what they're doing on the basis of his authority in such matters. Manifestations of power in teaching, healing, and exorcism, extend even to the Sabbath as Jesus portrays himself as its Lord.

The narrator next moves us into the synagogue to highlight a further Sabbath scene. Jesus has been in this synagogue before, and no doubt some of those attending had already experienced a manifestation of his teaching and exorcism power.

A man with a disabled hand enters the story. Tension must have been high as the synagogue becomes a scene of rising conflict. Healing on the Sabbath, in life-threatening circumstances was permitted, but it's unlikely this disabled man was in such a critical state.

Jesus takes the initiative with nothing less than a full public display – the man is singled out and healed. The question of healing is verbalized, and Jesus' exaggerated formulation receives no response. At this, Jesus expresses anger and deep grieving because of the hardness of their hearts – the man is healed, it seems almost as an aside, yet it is still another manifestation of Jesus' power and the nearness of the KOG.

The cumulative result of these stories of controversy and conflict is a growing plot against Jesus – the Pharisees and political pundits now want him dead, as they view him as a threat to their illegitimate power and authority.

3:7 - 35

Recall that Mark 2:1-3:6, comprises a series of five *controversy* stories about Jesus, throws light onto the growing contrast between the religious elite and the enthusiasm of the crowds. The overall positive crowd response to Jesus, as well as the authorities' suspicion and doubt concerning his actions and teachings, is in play. Who is this enigmatic and provocative character? Throughout Mark's story, Jesus faces opposition, which comes in the form of scribes 2:6; scribes of the Pharisees 2:16; the Pharisees 2:24; and the Pharisees and Herodians; 3:6.

The stories themselves expound on a healing and a dispute about forgiveness in 2:1-12; the calling of a disciple and a dispute over eating with sinners 2:13-17; a dispute over fasting giving rise to two provocative expositions by Jesus 2:18-22; a dispute over eating on the Sabbath 2:23-28; and a dispute over a healing on the Sabbath.

Our first two controversies deal with the acceptance of sinners and the last two with the Sabbath—the controversy in the middle, concerning fasting and Jesus' challenging sayings, is meant to function as a center piece that refers both back and forward, drawing the other disputes into the sphere of the truth of Jesus' self-identification and the transformative newness of his mission and proclamation of the KOG as it now radically reshapes Jewish belief. Jesus' words, deeds, and messages are aligned with the good news that the time is fulfilled, the KOG – the rule of God – has arrived.

As a result of the KOG arriving, there will be a shattering and redefining of the status quo. An invitation to those considered outside the realm of God's healing and forgiveness will be extended as well as a critique of the religious elite, who tend to see themselves as insiders and definers of the status quo.

It is important to note that these controversies with Jesus are structured in a manner that also comprises something of a cumulative trajectory. That is, by the time we arrive at the last of the five Galilean controversies in 3:1-6, the narrator reveals two unique results: the first is that Jesus is angry at the hardness of hearts present in the synagogue; and the second, that there are now those outside who are conspiring to destroy him. The latter, remember, was implied earlier in the text with Jesus' remark about the bridegroom being taken away.

God's good news inevitably brings disputes and controversy as the Son of Man, Lord of Sabbath, the bridegroom, Son of God, beloved Son, Holy One of God, Jesus of Nazareth breaks down the dividing barriers between people. He transforms the status quo through the embodiment of the good news of God's kingdom and all that it comprises – including the overthrow of evil, the forgiveness of sins, and the healing of the disenfranchised and destitute.

Notice that there are two levels of a *surplus of meaning* here. Jesus and the KOG don't have just 'one' meaning, or just 'any' meaning either. That is, Jesus comprises all the titles mentioned and more, while the KOG is both conceptual and imagical, related to and invoking a complex constellation of thoughts, feelings, and imaginative observations that God is reigning.

The next part of the story unfolds in 3:7-12, which takes the form of a narrative summary that pulls together a number of things, providing readers with a broad-based picture of the progression of the story up until now, while simultaneously paving the way for what is coming next.

In the previous summary back in 1:32-34, we were given the picture of the popularity of Jesus, mobbed by crowds, healer of the disabled, and exorciser of demons. This time we see Jesus' departure, his disciples, the swarming crowds, and his healings followed by the customary unclean spirits, who both recognize and acknowledge the truth of who Jesus is, something that Mark's readers – but not the characters in the story – have already been given insight into back in chapter 1. As seen previously, Jesus shuts down an untimely revealing of who he is by unclean spirits. What they know is not yet to be revealed in the context of the unfolding of his identity and mission, which continues to be a progressive unveiling of the KOG.

As we pick up the story again in chapter 3, verses 13-35, the narrator recounts several responses to Jesus in regards to being *insiders* or *outsiders* as the theme of reversal continues to manifest itself. Up to this point, there has been no formalizing of the disciples in the story. Jesus has, so far, called five to follow him and no doubt there are others, not specified doing the same.

Jesus goes up to the mountain—a place of frequent OT revelations and selects and appoints the twelve. He commissions them to be with him, to be sent out to proclaim the KOG, and to exorcise demons.

Jesus' formal choosing of twelve likely reflects the sociological context, rather than making a theological statement. The choice of twelve may also be a suggestion that the hoped-for restoration of Israel's twelve tribes is now taking on a new and transformative direction. The preparation for the transfer of Jesus' mission and message is now being set in motion, as the narrator bluntly points to his eventual betrayal by Judas. Amidst the 'insiders' then there is already an 'outsider.'

From the mountain, Jesus returns home. The narrator describes the scene, off the backdrop of the 'outsider' portrayal of Judas, in highly charged terms. The presence and pressure of the crowds were becoming so overwhelming that neither the disciples nor Jesus could eat.

Apparently, the news of all this furious activity reaches Jesus' family, who decides to come to Capernaum. Wild rumors are beginning to circulate concerning Jesus' activities, and his family decides it's time to bring him into line before things get even further out of control.

In verses 22-30 we now have a clear example of one of Mark's narrative strategies – interpolation. Namely, the story about the Jerusalem scribes is located within the story about Jesus' family and the wider theme of reversal and 'insiders' and 'outsiders' – integrating one story into another highlights them both.

We'll come back to the family considerations in verse 31 later – for now, let's focus on the accusation of the scribes. The forceful charges against Jesus are that he is possessed by Satan and that his exorcisms are taking place through the ruler of demons.

Jesus calls the scribes over and addresses their indictment through the device of skillfully perceptive and provoking sayings – parables. In verses 23b to 27, he negates the absurdity of the scribes' perspective, leading them to draw out the conclusions of their fool hardy logic. Far from Jesus' exorcisms being the result of possession by Satan or having the power of the ruler of demons, he indicates that Satan's kingdom is under attack. Jesus is raiding what had become Satan's territory and transforming it into his own.

Jesus, by analogy, in verse 27, offers the perspective that he has not only entered the territory of Satan, but that he is rescuing those under his regime of oppression. He is bringing salvation through the coming KOG, which comprises conflict, reversal, and power battles through which God is establishing his reign.

From parables, Jesus moves into a sharp and direct warning – "Amen, I say to you." He begins markedly setting himself up in an authoritative position, which no other Jewish teacher would dare claim as their own. People will be forgiven, he says, for their sins, but anyone who blasphemes the Holy Spirit has no forgiveness in this age and is liable to everlasting consequences. What is unforgivable here is to allege that the mark of God through the Spirit (recall Jesus' reception of the Spirit for the empowering of his mission back in 1:10-13) is a manifestation of the power of evil; to attribute to Satan what is of God. This is a rejection of the truth of the arrival of the kingdom and who Jesus is as both its inaugurator and proclaimer.

Jesus' warning, therefore, is explicitly aimed at any who make a deliberate choice to attribute what God is doing to evil, or as actions possessed by the evil one. And just in case readers fail to grasp the point, the narrator repeats the accusation of the scribes in verse 30. Jesus, they assume, has an unclean spirit, no doubt a play on the Holy Spirit as mentioned in the previous verse.

In some Christian circles the notion of the 'unforgivable sin,' be it for victim or victimizer, is usually an ocean length's distance of the mark. I've heard it used in such a diversity of contexts, to instill fear in others or to harbor it in oneself, but most of the time the contexts have nothing to do with Jesus' saying here – and this is the only place it occurs in the text.

The narrator brings us back, in verses 31-35, to the previous story concerning Jesus' family who may now have serious questions about his sanity. The link between this family story and that of the scribes is to show the various developing attitudes and responses to Jesus – there will be a contrast between 'insiders' and 'outsiders' whether this is the religious elite from Jerusalem, family from Nazareth, or the twelve.

The narrator's concern is with response and direction. In short, Jesus is stressing the importance of being part of a new family – that which may or may not include one's fidelity to the religious elite or one's natural family. If family conflicts related to following Jesus should arise, there may be painful decisions to make, but the Markan narrator has no space to undertake such issues or to offer a balanced perspective as to how such issues should be resolved.

In this scene, Jesus' mother and brothers are portrayed as *outside*, while the crowd is *inside* with Jesus. The crowd informs Jesus of the family visit and repeats what the narrator wants us to envision – the family is *outside*. Jesus' reply to the crowd around him at first seems absurd – who are my mother and brothers?

One would assume that those around Jesus may have begun to wonder if he was indeed losing his mind. They may have surmised, but, of course, "your mother and brother are outside." The narrator, however, has other interests than pursuing this line of thought. Assumptions need to be checked and verified. Jesus looks at those *inside* around him and now brings a significantly new meaning to the idea of family. Those, he says, who are *inside* around him are his mother and brothers. He follows this with the saying, "whoever does the will of God is his brother, sister, and mother." Jesus' new confirmation of family is not based on one's assumptions of belonging, but in the context of the story, as seen back in 1:14-15, it is connected to his inaugurating the KOG, therefore calling for repentance and belief in the good news. To reject this call, as Jesus' natural family and the scribes from Jerusalem were in danger of doing, is to situate oneself *outside* the will of God as it is now being proclaimed and acted out by the Son of Man.

4:1 – 34

In the first chapter of this story, the narrator has presented the character Jesus in Galilee as proclaiming the good news of God – of announcing the time is fulfilled – stating that the KOG is near. After these pronouncements, one of the most pressing aims of the narrative is to develop a series of incidents that show readers something of the identity and authority of Jesus in the midst of conflict and suspense.

Principally, in these early chapters of Mark's story Jesus tells people to follow him, and they follow, he orders demons to depart, and they depart, and he commands people to be healed, and they are healed – pretty astounding stuff.

All of these authoritative gestures performed by Jesus, and the contexts in which they take place, raised a fair amount of controversy and attention, causing the Pharisees and the political pundits of the day to want to destroy him. Jesus was an enigmatic figure – unclean spirits know who he is, 1:24 and 3:11, while his followers' plight seems to be that they are always trying, not very successfully, to figure him out.

After the scribes accusation of Jesus' casting out unclean spirits by the power of Satan and his parabolic response in 3:23-27 that this suggestion is absurd, we see the clear contrast, at this point in the story at 3:31-35 of those "outside" and those "inside" and that whoever does God's will is "inside."

In approaching chapter four, with the previous preface in mind, we will discern that the narrator has put together a further series of Jesus' teaching, in parables, to continue to highlight his authority and to reveal his identity gradually.

Recall that in addition to healing and exorcising unclean spirits, Jesus is challenging old ways of thinking and understanding. He releases people from sin, eats with sinners, doesn't fast, ignores Sabbath regulations, and is suspected to have lost his mind. No wonder his notoriety was fast spreading throughout the whole region.

Jesus then is attracting large crowds of people, and this is where we pick up the story in chapter four. Notice that there are so many in the crowd that Jesus takes refuge in a boat, in all likelihood so that as many as possible could hear his teaching.

So, then picture the scene – huge crowd of people – Jesus in a boat about to teach in parables and the first thing he says is: "Listen! Hear!"

The next scene in verse 10 now abruptly shifts to Jesus being alone with "those around him" and the twelve disciples. Note that in the previous chapter at verses 32 and 34 "those around him" are insiders – those who are part of Jesus' true family because they are considered to be those who do the will of God. In these verses, Jesus doesn't seem to exclude those outside being able to join his true family, as he says "whoever," in verse 35, but his stress is on affirming that those around him are his true family.

Remember, furthermore, that Jesus has already, earlier in chapter three, spoken parables to the scribes who accused him of purging unclean spirits by the power of Satan. Returning to verse 10 now, those around Jesus and the twelve as insiders ask about parables.

The twelve and those around him then are interested in Jesus and his parables, whereas apparently the rest of the large crowd has little curiosity and therefore merely *hear* parables without any benefit – otherwise they would have followed Jesus and been around him.

Jesus' reply to the curious is that they have been given the secret mystery of the KOG. In other words, God's kingship is so radically other, which will become more clearly evident later, that its revealing depends on God's action and not human speculation.

Next, Jesus refers to those outside, who by contrast to those around him and the twelve inside, everything comes in parables. Outsiders, on the story level here, are likely to be firstly those scribes who accused Jesus of purging unclean spirits by the power of Satan, who remember were spoken to in parables back in 3:23, secondly, those who may assume they're inside, but view Jesus as having lost his mind 3:21 and 31-32, and thirdly those who heard Jesus' parables, but didn't really listen to the points of interest with curiosity – parables, for them, were like a joke without a punch line – they could take them or leave them.

Jesus' parables, it seems, could compel or repel, and for those who ignore his challenge to "Listen," to be able to hear really, the result will be that parables turn on them. Accusations against Jesus will have the effect of subterfuge, which will disable true hearing about him and the good news of the KOG. The crucial emphasis falls on how one is hearing – if it's with disinterested apathetic ears, then the message of Jesus will repel, rather than compel curiosity about who he is and what the KOG is revealing.

A final point worth touching on seems to me to be that the narrative itself leaves Jesus' relationship to insiders and outsiders quite open. Sometimes outsiders became insiders, other times, as we will see later, especially in the case of Judas, insiders became outsiders. This is to say that the narrative seems to leave these groups of people somewhat flexible or changeable. Jesus' charge is, "Let anyone with ears to hear – listen."

The explanation of the parable of the soils goes some way in alerting readers that there will be differing responses to Jesus. Ironically, these insiders who have been given the mystery (secret) of the KOG need to understand.

The sower sows the logos – the word, but in the first group of people Satan – Jesus' enemy in the clash of kingdoms – takes it away. The penetration of the word is so superficial in these people that their response is negligible and all too easily disappears.

And then there are those whose response begins well, but rapidly fades, especially in cases of difficulties. And then thirdly some people show greater sustainability in their response to the word, yet are enticed away to other things with the result that the word is minimized and utterly unproductive in their lives. Lastly, we have those who are good soil. They hear, then accept and then bear fruit in response to the word. The extravagance of the yield is astronomical – absolutely shocking. In all likelihood, we return, in verses 21-32, to the larger crowd who now take in a selection of Jesus' parables.

The first two are rather enigmatic riddles. Light is meant to illuminate not be tempered, and anything undisclosed to be disclosed. We might say it this way: revealing opens up the possibility of finding that which previously remained unillumined or hidden.

Next, hearers of parables are again challenged to listen. Jesus incites hearers to hear carefully and attentively: again, how they hear is crucial. He uses the language of everyday life that usually centers on equality in the proverbial measuring. The saying here, however, seems to indicate something like: the more curious hearer of Jesus' parables you are, the more you will get out of them. So, for the interested hearer, there will be more than a mere equality or return. The result of this response is that if you have received something from parables, you will be given even more, whereas the indifferent, apathetic, and disinterested who have received nothing from them, will end up with nothing at all.

These two parables connect with the earlier part of this chapter and stress Jesus' identity and authority in parables - he is revealer and concealer, depending on the response people have to him and his teaching.

The last two parables in verses 26-32 concern more directly the KOG and both pick up the previously mentioned metaphor of seed.

In the first parable, the KOG is extravagantly like the seed that is randomly strewn around, grows on its own, becomes ripe, and ready for harvest. Despite what may appear to be an improbable case – most farmers wouldn't agree – the KOG is active; it has a destiny God will bring about.

In the second parable, the KOG is like a tiny seed that eventually grows into a large shrub. At first, God's kingdom is a quite small and perhaps seemingly insignificant activity, but its final dimension will be extravagantly shocking in comparison to its beginning.

These two parables, each in their way, alert hearers to listen – to hear again rightly – the KOG is and will be an activity that is unexpected and surprising – it may seem ineffective or irrelevant, yet it is there and will reach its destiny in due time.

The narrator now returns to the story in verses 33-34 with another summary. This time it is informing readers that parables were a regular type of teaching that Jesus continued to practice in many contexts.

Considering the rest of the chapter, it seems likely that the narrator wants to underline that Jesus' parables bring forth different responses – for those who respond with curiosity and interest; they reveal, which leads to more explanation, while for others who are indifferent and uninterested; they conceal, and lead to nothing.

4:35 – 5:43 (1)

Following the report of Jesus' teaching in parables, the narrator moves on to the end of the day to now prepare the reader for a further demonstration of Jesus' identity and authority. His desire to go to the other side of the lake is not explained, merely stated. Perhaps, he was seeking rest and time farther away from the crowds.

At some point, during the crossing, a storm arises on the lake, and one of the boats is in danger of sinking. Jesus is asleep but awakened by those in his boast who assume they are going to drown.

Jesus' panic ridden followers awaken him with the question – "Teacher, you care that we are perishing don't you?" Just then Jesus responds by stilling the wind and calming the sea. Here we have the first story of Jesus' power manifestations in connection with nature. Such manifestations can take place because the world is both natural and spiritual. Let's say that it comprises at least two dimensions and maybe more, of one reality. Jesus knows how the world operates. Once the storm is mastered, he turns to his followers and poses two questions: Why fear and where is your faith? Jesus' remarkable and unfolding authority is shocking and insiders – the curious and interested who are following him – are gradually learning more about who he is and just how far the scope of his authority goes.

Neither of these questions finds a response on the narrative level, but what readers are given insight into is that those in the boat experience greater fear concerning the extent of Jesus' manifestation of power, than they express about drowning. Instead of answering Jesus, they ask each other, who then can this possibly be that has mastery over the wind and sea? The followers of Jesus, presently insiders, are getting a clearer glimpse of who it is they are engaged with and because of this what masterful authority he has for manifesting the KOG.

As Jesus' questions have gone unanswered on the narrative level, so too it seems will the question of his followers. Yet, as the story moves on something of a response is forthcoming, but it is somewhat shocking, in that it comes from a most unlikely source, which we will discover in just a moment. Having arrived safely on the other side of the sea and into Gentile territory the scene unfolds for a dramatic encounter with a man who has an unclean spirit. Recall that the narrative has just recounted a short story about Jesus' power and authority over wind and sea; now he is going to be facing a potent demonic who may represent death itself.

The narrator confirms this with a fairly high level of description concerning the man. He is living among tombs, unable to be bound, even with a chain, which used to have some success, then he was put in shackles, but to no avail – nothing and no one can master his strength. The unclean spirit is a force of destruction in this poor man's life. He's constantly beating himself under the relentless possession; he howls in anguish night and day.

And then this powerful force runs toward Jesus, rather than away from him. Not only this, but he bows before Jesus shouting, "Why do you interfere with me, Jesus, Son of the Most High God?" We have here then a partial answer to the question posed earlier by Jesus' followers in spite of the somewhat pagan associations that "Most High God" may have carried in Gentile territory.

At any rate, Jesus superiority is clearly acknowledged, yet there is a sense of demonic maneuvering to take control of the encounter and Jesus. Notice that ironically, the unclean spirit appeals to Jesus via God, to be left alone.

Apparently, according to verse 8, Jesus had already attempted to purge the man of the unclean spirit, but to no avail. By the narrator's inclusion of this attempt here, in all likelihood, he wants to stress that this was no ordinary exorcism, and also perhaps, to show that Jesus' encounters with unclean spirits were not always first strike successes.

And then Jesus takes a further initiative confirming his superiority by forcing out the name of the unclean spirit, which in turn heightens the drama, as we find out that Jesus is facing not just one unclean spirit, but an array of them. This may explain the narrator's earlier description of the inabilities of anyone to control this person. His life is inflicted and possessed by strange and reprehensible forces.

The divulging of the name *Legion* and the reality that this encounter is not with one unclean spirit quickly turns to the multitude of unclean spirits pleading through the man not to be relocated, perhaps for fear of lacking human possession to make themselves apparent.

They seem to recognize that Jesus has authority over their fate and therefore request the alternative of being sent into a herd of pigs. As another sign of his authority, Jesus permits this – with the coming out the spirits enter the pigs and in keeping with their aims of destruction contribute to their drowning, although the destiny of the unclean spirits remains a question mark in this context.

What is of primary importance for the narrator comes next: the reaction. First, the herdsmen take flight, no doubt because of the disappearance of their pigs and perhaps to inform those whom they supply of this shocking event. Second, after this, people *come* and *see* what happened. Third, they come to Jesus and see the demonic manifesting all the signs of healing in contrast to chain breaking, pounding himself with stones, and shouting – remember the narrator suggests this is the man who was under the influence and possession of a multiplicity of unclean spirits. Fourth, after coming and seeing their response is fear. They are so shocked by coming and seeing – they neither respond to the man or are curious to know more about Jesus.

Next, those who were present tell the crowd more to confirm the authenticity of the encounter, exorcism, and destruction of the herd. Fifth, as the unclean spirits pleaded with Jesus previously, now the people plead with him to leave their vicinity. The narrator wants readers to recognize that Jesus is not one to be ordered about and he will come and go according to his agenda and destiny.

Without any questions or confrontation, the narrator skips to the scene of Jesus getting into the boat, implying his willingness to comply with the pleas of the people and leave Gentile territory. But just then the evidently radically changed man pleads to be with Jesus. The refusal and command to "Go home" seem to be for the positive reasons of giving testimony to his friends and family regarding the authority and mercy he had been shown.

And then the man, as the narrator reports, goes away. His testimony, notice, far exceeds Jesus' command and the narrator wants readers to know that in the Decapolis, a Gentile territory made up of ten cities, the powerful impact of Jesus' action is proclaimed and all are amazed. It is worth noting at this stage of the story that Jesus' command to the ex-demoniac comes as something of a surprise. Recall back in chapter 1:40-45 where Jesus immediately heals a man with a skin disease. He is charged to say nothing to anyone and to follow ritual obligations concerning his reintegration into society.

The contrast in our story here is remarkable and may have to do with where the stories are geographically located – the first one on Jewish ground in Galilee – the second in Gentile territory. In one context, there is silence, in the other, proclamation (although this contrast is not always in force). It seems likely that Jesus is much more reticent in the Jewish milieu. There is a greater risk of a misunderstanding who he is and what his mission is out to accomplish, whereas Gentiles had little information about a messiah figure and therefore such misunderstandings were less likely and if they did exist would not reach the fervor of Jewish expectation.

4:35 – 5:43 (2)

In the last chapters, we further explored something of the aims and identity of Jesus of Nazareth. At the end of chapter 4, we saw that part of Jesus' identity is that he is one who has mastery over winds and waters. His rather faithless followers are astonished and shocked by his manifestations of power, which leads them to begin to ask each other who, then, is this that even the wind and sea obey him?

Seeing that this incident takes place during the crossing of the sea when arriving at the destination safely, another challenge immediately faces Jesus. He tangles with a well-known man who has an unclean spirit or rather, what turns out to be a multiplicity of these spirits. Notice the narrator's lengthy description of the state of this poor man again, but also notice how quickly readers are told that he bows before Jesus, who has already, apparently unsuccessfully, commanded the unclean spirits to come out. Yet, exorcism, even of what turns out to be multiple unclean spirits, is not beyond Jesus' manifestations of power – giving readers another clue to his true identity. Jesus' mastery extends, not only to wind and water, but his power is capable of exorcising multiple unclean spirits, when no one else could deal with the poor man living in the tombs.

Furthermore, it seems that the narrator wants to give readers in 5:1 "on the other side" a glimpse into Jesus' unfolding missional trajectory into Gentile territory, as the notorious outsiders, at least in some Jewish eyes, are going to be invited in. Not only do most Jewish hearers need a new understanding of Jesus as Messiah, but non-Jews do as well. Recounting Jesus' actions, teaching, and power manifestations is a formidable narrative task. The intrigue of the story and that to which it points readers intends to refigure lives for those who are willing to read and be read by the text.

We go on in Mark's story starting at 5:21. Jesus is going to cross back over to the other side of the lake and into Jewish territory. On this recounting, there is a huge crowd around him. In contrast to being asked, as previously, to vacate the premises, this shows that his immense popularity had not diminished and why people were still attracted to him for various reasons.

Jairus, an important figure in the synagogue, arrives on the scene. Intriguingly, like the Legion, the people, and the exorcised man earlier in this chapter, Jairus pleads, or better, pleads repeatedly; acknowledging Jesus' power and authority to heal his dear daughter.

Jesus turns and sets out with Jairus, while the crowd pushes and jostles to fold into him. Just then, with the daughter of Jairus dying, the narrator interpolates a long series of phrases describing a woman's desperate plight. She had been bleeding for twelve years, which would have meant she was ritually unclean and therefore an outcast in her community. This poor woman had tried everything available to be cured and now had no money left. Jesus' reputation was growing wildly and the woman no doubt has heard of his power and authority. After the narrator informs readers that she has touched the clothes of Jesus, her faith and trust that Jesus could heal are revealed. At once the woman's fountain of blood dries up, and her physical and psychological hemorrhaging ceases. Twelve years of ineffective treatment, while Jesus' power manifestation, unleashed by the woman's faith, can cure her immediately and permanently. The narrator reports that she felt the flow of blood stop and recognized she was healed.

At once Jesus realizes that his power to heal having been manifested, has a referent which is clear from his question: Who touched my clothes? In a subtle, yet radical way, the narrator is heightening the reader's perspective of Jesus as a fully performant power broker with a power identity – even touching him unleashes healing.

The disciples, perhaps not as clued in as readers, respond to Jesus' question by stating the obvious. Lots of people are pressing in on him. Why should he ask who touched him? The narrator's unwillingness to critique the disciples' ignorance at this stage intends to throw attention back on the action of Jesus. After a pause, where Jesus looks around, the woman comes before him as she would a king. Her fear and trembling are likely to be a description of a reaction to the powerful Jesus and the fact that this power has now manifested itself in her life making her well. She then tells Jesus all the truth, perhaps including here her story of twelve years of suffering as well as her daring risk, in faith, to touch him.

Jesus' response to the woman brings this power story and the narrator's interpolation to a close. His reference to her as "daughter" may further portray Jesus in an authoritative light, while also being a sign of his compassionate welcoming her into his new family, which as we have seen previously in this narrative, is made up of those who follow Jesus and do the will of God (3:35). Doing the will of God, in this woman's context, was having faith that Jesus had power to heal her. "Go in peace," he tells her, confirming and assuming that from then on, her disease was cured.

Lest we, as readers, have forgotten: what is going on behind the scenes of Jesus' healing of the bleeding woman? Now, the narrator brings us back to the matter at hand: Jairus' daughter, who, when we started her story after Jesus returned to the Jewish side of the sea, was dying.

At this point, in verse 35, people come to Jairus to inform him that his daughter is now dead, so there is no use in Jesus attending to the girl. But Jesus, who may have been near Jairus, overhears the devastating news. He responds to, as the narrator reminds us, an important figure in the Jewish synagogue – "Don't fear; only believe." That is, Jesus takes charge. His power skills are about to face the ultimate challenge, but he announces he is up to the task at hand. As was the case with the faith of the bleeding woman previously, if Jairus believes Jesus has the power to save his daughter, she will live.

We are offered no narrative explanation as to why Jesus permits only the three disciples, Peter, James, and John, to follow him. This trio may be privileged to participate because they will at some later stage play a significant role in giving testimony to Jesus' actions, than any other disciples. At any rate, the narrator makes more of the mourners carrying on, as this will highlight the drama and Jesus' power to bring the dead girl back to life. Jesus' question and statement shows as much. Why all this death behavior? The little child has not died, but is sleeping. Jesus' question and statement provoke laughter, with the unmentioned underlying assumption that they think he has gotten it quite wrong.

Authoritatively, Jesus excuses the mourners sending them outside, while he turns and takes inside the parents and the three disciples. The stage is now set for Jesus' ultimate power confrontation with defilement and death. Notice Jesus' actions are far from those of Hellenistic magicians with their incantations or ritual formulas. Very simply he takes the little child's hand, defying ritual uncleanliness, and then tells her to arise. And immediately or at once, one of the narrator's favorite terms, she does. Jesus' power to restore life to the little girl is instant. There is no time lag or waiting for her to arise. Her walking around affirms the point: Jesus has power even over death. Who indeed can this be?

Those in the room are astonishingly astonished. The magnitude of astonishment matches, in some sense, Jesus' power. It is great. Strangely, or at first, so it seems, Jesus commands the witnesses of this manifestation of power not to let anyone know about it, and to give the little girl some food. If anything were more obvious, it would be unlikely – that is, to let everyone know she is alive and to feed the girl would seem to be the normal course of events. What the narrator recounts here may serve a dual purpose. First, Jesus could be requiring silence, to slip away without further ado – the healing of the bleeding woman and the restoring of life to the little girl may have been too much for the growing crowds that Jesus would have had to make his way through to depart. He says something like – keep quiet for now so I can leave the scene and return home without extraordinary problems. Further, what makes this a likely scenario is that any such manifestation of power, as Jesus has just performed, would have been impossible to keep a secret for long.

The second purpose suits the little girl – that she should eat would be a pretty straightforward conclusion – but Jesus joins this to his departure, implying that the girl should eat before the mourners and eventual crowds discover she is alive. In both cases there is a delay – one so Jesus can go on his way without problems and the other so that the girl can regain her strength before facing the amazement of the crowd. The interpolating of these two specific healing power manifestations of Jesus, adds to the growing suspense surrounding his aims and identity.

Furthermore, the bleeding woman – an outsider and one who was ritually unclean – and a leader of the synagogue – an insider and one who was ritually clean, creates a skillfully told and ironic contrast, where the woman ends up paving the way of faith in Jesus' power, for the synagogue leader who is instructed not to fear, only to have faith. Remarkably, Jesus' manifestations of power now go even beyond winds and water and these two stories within the wider narrative context, show readers he can heal the most dreadful diseases and has power over death itself.

6:1 - 30

The Markan narrative from chapters 1-5 is geographically centered in Galilee. Jesus' manifestations of power and his teaching have touched Jews and Gentiles in the region of Capernaum and around the Sea of Galilee. The success of his mission, in spite of conflict, has been remarkable. Lest readers fall into a false sense of security, however, the story now opens up another angle.

As we arrive at chapter 6 the location shifts and along with it so does our understanding of Jesus. Jesus leaves Jairus and his family and comes to Nazareth, his hometown, with the disciples following. While the disciples play no role in the Nazareth scene, they will become an important feature of the narrative in the following scenario.

We find Jesus teaching in the synagogue on the Sabbath. On this occasion, the narrator forgoes saying anything about the context of the teaching and focuses readers on its effect. Those in the synagogue who heard Jesus' teaching were astonished. Up until now, Jesus' appearances in synagogues have primarily been scenes of manifestations of power in exorcisms or healings. Responses to these acts of power have changed – from amazement, with the result that Jesus' fame spreads – to conflict, which sets in motion a conspiracy to destroy him.

This time hearers react to the teaching in the synagogue with a series of pejoratively slanted questions. Their queries begin to reveal their suspicion. They have little real interest in the identity of Jesus. The synagogue hearers, in this scene, are wondering how a local man like Jesus can say and do what he does. Our first questions raise the issue of origin – where do these things come from? This implies that a normal guy like Jesus has to be getting his wisdom and power from a source other than himself. After all, as the next queries illuminate, Jesus is a well-known regular guy from a familiar family like many others in the region. It is probable, though not explicitly stated, that the narrator's aim is for readers to recall two previous scenes; first, that Jesus has been accused previously of being associated with unclean spirits and of receiving his authority from Satan. Jesus resoundingly refuted the charges, but those synagogue hearers would not know what readers do. And the second scene is where Jesus receives the spirit empowering him for the task at hand, which was to overthrow Satan and to perform and proclaim the arrival of the KOG – and both scenes will finally lead him to his crucifixion. The synagogue audience, though astounded, takes no notice of the possibility that Jesus may have a new family and a new identity. Suspicion gets the better of trust, which results in their taking offense at him or being tripped up or entrapped by their unbelief.

Suspicion and unbelief lead Jesus to proclaim a truism: a prophet is often rejected by his own, to which the narrator adds: manifestations of power were rare in contrast to the profusion of previous exorcisms and healings. And Jesus marvels at their unbelief, as all he is doing is creating possibilities for appropriate trust to defeat inappropriate suspicion.

The next scene opens outside of Nazareth where Jesus is now teaching. At this point, the disciples are reintroduced into the storyline as the twelve who will be sent out to extend Jesus' mission and represent his authority, in particular, over unclean spirits.

This is followed by some travel orders about what to take and not take for the task at hand. The narrator may be following the pre-Exodus tradition in Exodus 12; just as the Jews were going to be sent out from Egypt, as an expression of God's kingdom, so now the disciples are doing the same. Only the bare minimum is necessary. Jesus reminds the twelve that they should expect a mixed response to their activities on his behalf. Some will accept them, while others will not.

The narrator reports that after receiving their commission the disciples go out, adding this time, that they do so with the proclamation - preaching of repentance, and extending Jesus' authority over unclean spirits and healing many. This confirmation aims to show the spread of Jesus' manifestations of power through the sent out ones to many who are in need of being liberated from possession, diverse ailments, and diseases.

The next part of the story is a good example of interpolation - inserting one story in the midst of another (see Introduction). On this occasion, the narrator fills out the story and destiny of John the baptizer that was left fairly undeveloped back in chapter 1. One of the reasons for the lack of development there, in my view, is that the narrator senses the urgency of getting readers straight into the character of Jesus. It does not serve their purpose, or that of the story, to take the time at the outset of chapter 1, to get into any more detail about John. Jesus is the central character in the plot, and the narrator wastes no time pointing readers in his direction. Assuming that this is a fair assessment of not going into detail about John in chapter 1 how does the story and its gruesome details fit any better into this stage of the narrative?

It seems to me there are at least two reasons to insert this story into the story about the sending out of the twelve. First, the narrator wants to inform readers about the hostile context that the disciples, and ultimately Jesus, have to face. That is, the interpolation of this story at this point is to portray an atmosphere – its aim and information are atmospherical. The narrator wants readers to feel the chilling presence of political opposition and the tragic consequences that those in power can inflict upon anyone who might challenge their authority. John, for now, is the primary example.

A second reason to insert this story here is to highlight the breadth of Jesus' mission and authority extended through the twelve. Jesus' activities have raised conflicts and questions, and new readers can recognize the extent of Jesus' prolific presence as awareness of his name has even reached Herod Antipas himself. That is to say – Jesus' notoriety is growing and the twelve have an evident role in spreading his authority and mission.

Notice the narrator begins the story with a focus on 'why' Herod hears. Jesus' name and manifestations of power are creating high levels of interest and a fair amount of speculation concerning his identity. His reputation was now becoming more well-known, and people were assessing some different possibilities as to who he was: John raised from the dead, Elijah, a prophet of those of old – Herod's view is that he is John – whom he beheaded – that has been raised.

The rest of the story does a number of things: it shows the reason for John's imprisonment and eventual death; it portrays John as willing to challenge corrupt political authority and affirms he was righteous and holy; it reveals that Herod was fearful of John and furthermore he may have had some serious questions about Jesus as he viewed him as John raised from the dead.

The high degree of narrative detail in this story aims to highlight the unmistakable truth of John's gruesome death. But this is to be situated in the broader context of the sending out of the twelve, who contribute to the spread of Jesus' authority and mission in the increasingly uncertain times, and also in the retrospective of Herod's presumption that Jesus is John raised from the dead. Rumors about Jesus' power manifestations and growing influence must have been startling enough for Herod to conclude that this option seemed best to explain who Jesus was.

The narrator next returns to the 'sent out ones' in verse 30, looking back to verse 7. They came together with Jesus to confirm the passing on of his power and authority, but this leaves readers with a rather fragile sense of success, considering the backdrop of John's execution. As readers of the story, at this stage, we are left within the unfolding drama that highlights three things:

First, those who are astounded by Jesus' teaching and manifestations of power, yet are scandalized at him, so much so, that these questions aim to negate the very possibility that Jesus might be someone other than the person they have assumed he is. To be scandalized by Jesus may produce various responses. In this case, in contrast to the numerous previous occasions of belief, it is unbelief.

Second, the role of the twelve now comes more clearly into focus. They are sent out ones who spread the call to repent in light of Jesus' mission and ministry. Receiving authority from Jesus to heal and cast out unclean spirits, they set a new context for the unfolding transmission of the KOG and the widespread acclaim of Jesus of Nazareth. The disciples' role in the drama will continue to grow, as will their understanding of Jesus and the truth of his identity, authority, and mission.

Third, as the mission is undertaken, readers are not to be overly optimistic. As the political atmosphere is set against it, by inserting the story of John's beheading, the narrator wants readers to feel the sense of the crushing power ploys of Herod's political tyranny, and the new context of the high level of risk for both Jesus and the disciples' mission on his behalf. The complication here is that Jesus and the disciples are a threat to those who are in authority – the political pundits, who wield the sword in their own favor set a chilling atmosphere for the ongoing mission, underlying the clash of kingdoms yet to come as the story continues to unfold.

6:30 – 7:23

Following the sending out of the twelve and the marking of the occasion by the atmospheric recounting of the gruesome story about John's beheading, alerting readers to the unjust political power and its threat to Jesus' mission, the sent out ones return to Jesus and give a report of their doings and teachings.

The narrator gives readers no indication of Jesus' response; approval or disapproval, but merely shows his pastoral concern for this group of followers, by suggesting they take a rest. This attempt to escape the crowds and to find a quiet place opens on to the next scene. The crowds not only follow the boat's journey, but people arrive before Jesus, and the disciples reach their destination. Thoughts of rest and quiet are quickly replaced by crowd identification, which deftly characterizes it as, in similarity to many OT contexts, a leaderless and uncared for group of people. Jesus' compassion results in his taking an extended time to teach them. Notice that for Jesus, compassion in this context is first connected to providing the crowd with needed direction and insight concerning its wandering ways.

Some long hours of teaching result in the disciples suggesting that Jesus send the people away for something to eat. His response to the disciples is both shocking and bewildering. Shocking to think so much food could be bought, and bewildering because they are in a remote place where having plenty of money would have no significance for the task at hand. The disciples, however, not knowing where this is going, are ready and willing literally to carry out Jesus' instructions. Just then, he interjects, with a question to which his disciples respond noting their meager supplies. After the disciples' response, Jesus takes authoritative action ordering them to organize and divide the crowd in a formation. After this,

Jesus takes the small supply of loaves and fish and gives thanks, breaking the bread and distributing it with the fish, through the disciples.

Remarkably, Jesus' implied manifestation of power results in everyone eating to their fill and the disciples collecting what was left over. Only the disciples, and not the crowd, are aware of what has just taken place. The narrator's mention of five thousand may be a hint of rising messianic fervor in the region, but Jesus teaches and feeds, rather than giving military orders. While this story characteristically throws further light on a response to the question of Jesus' identity, it also subtly suggests the disciples are gradually becoming more a part of Jesus' mission, yet they too have not understood who he is, or what he is out to accomplish. Our next scenario highlights both those elements, as the story moves on.

Not without some abruptness, Jesus urgently sends the disciples on their way. What kinds of messianic concoctions were being thrown around in the crowd is anyone's guess. At any rate, the disciples leave in some haste, the crowd is sent away, and Jesus leaves, departing to a mountain to pray.

The narrator next, in verses 45-52, portrays a picture of the disciples, in a boat on the lake, sometime around 3-6 AM. They're working hard, but getting nowhere – they are failing to make headway, but do not appear to be in grave danger. Jesus then comes to them as God had previously appeared to people in theophanies in the OT.

When the disciples see Jesus walking on the lake, they assume they are seeing a ghost and are gripped by fear. Jesus' mastery over the natural world, as previously highlighted in chapter 4, again takes center stage as he not only calms raging winds and seas, but now he walks on a lake and joins his disciples in the boat.

With the same urgency as noted in verse 45, Jesus tells them to be strong and not to fear, as it is indeed he and not a ghost who is joining them. Jesus' authority and its results thoroughly amaze the disciples, yet just as remarkably the narrator now informs readers that the disciples' astonishment at the power manifestation of Jesus actually confirms their ongoing misunderstanding of his identity, not picked up in the previous provision of food for five thousand, and this due to their hard-heartedness.

Meanwhile, after recounting these two striking accounts of Jesus' powerful activities, the disciples and Jesus arrive at Gennesaret, not the intended destination, but one nevertheless that shows, in the fifth summary of the narrative, the rising popularity and ongoing manifestations of power performed by Jesus.

At this point in the story, beginning in chapter 7, Pharisees and scribes from Jerusalem re-enter the scene. Formerly, back in chapter 3, a similar group of the pietistic minded Jewish leadership accuses Jesus of casting out unclean spirits by the power of the prince of demons. This time the supposed keepers of the law, those who were to guard Jewish orthodoxy, have serious questions about Jesus' disciples eating food without first washing their hands. The narrator's remarks in verses 3-4 are an indication that non-Jewish readers are certainly part of the target narrative audience and subsequently Jesus, after this interaction with the Jewish religious elite, will move off into Gentile territory. So, in verse 5, the question is raised. Jesus is asked why his followers are not keeping tradition and eating, most likely the leftovers from the previous story, without washing.

There is no doubt that in first century Judaism ritual food laws were one of the badges of Jewish distinctiveness and notoriety. For Pharisees and scribes, especially from Jerusalem, abandoning dietary laws would have been to desecrate Jewish status as the people of God. This then is a serious matter that carries strong implications concerning the authenticity of Jesus' attitudes to God and the law.

In the next sequence of verses, up to verse 15, the narrator recounts Jesus' response. Wasting no time, he quickly aims to turn the tables. Beautifully, as Isaiah put it so well, he surmises, you the formidable guardians of orthodoxy are a bunch of hypocrites. Why? Because at the core of this issue is an erosion of God's law and a prioritizing embrace of their traditions, in its place.

Even more pointed is the sarcastic irony of verse 9, which indicts the guardians of orthodoxy as setting aside God's commands for what amounts to their benefit. Notice that the illustration that follows attempts to show how this kind of thing takes place. In other words, there were several clever ways devised to protect one's possessions and property so that they would not have to be shared in any way with one's parents. Not only do such guardians of orthodoxy practice this type of subterfuge, but they pass it on to others as orthodoxy. Furthermore, this was just one example among many that Jesus could have appealed to in order to make his case.

Today in the church, unfortunately, many wave the banner of "we're orthodox believers, and you're not," without carefully examining and assessing whether their assumptions are justified. In fact, they may be the ones doing what they accuse others of doing; that is, prioritizing human tradition.

As the story now goes on, the Jerusalem guardians disappear, and the scene changes to the crowd being addressed by Jesus. He moves from the previous altercation with the religious elite on the way food was to be eaten to teaching the crowd about what to eat. Jesus' authoritative response to the Pharisees and scribes and his parabolic statement here about clean and unclean, challenge the whole notion of what defiles – unwashed hands or consuming certain foods – Jesus says this is not the core of the issue.

As the audience changes from the religious elite to the crowd, the crowd now dissipates, to give way to the disciples. They cannot make sense of the puzzling remarks of Jesus. Food, for example, when ingested has nothing to do with being clean as it goes through the stomach not the heart, and then into the toilet.

The heart, understood here to be the essential component of who one is, remains the central focus of Jesus. In this case, he authoritatively revises and points to the fulfillment of God's law in favor of a standard that situates the question of defilement as something that originates inside a person – the heart – and not be due to what a person consumes. The narrator, notice, interprets this as Jesus' affirmation that all foods are clean and therefore implies in a quite revolutionary manner that one's relation to God is not something based on the food one eats. The real culprit of that which is unclean originates inside a person – in the center of who one is. Thus, if defilement takes place, the proper context for understanding it is the state or condition of the heart.

As the church, we desperately need to be attuned to this important perspective. *Heart over hands.* Many church contexts today are wracked by division, while others embrace highly influential personality cults who focus on being the supposed guardians of orthodoxy. Sadly, there is a neglect of the heart, and a concern to inspect everyone else's hands. This is a serious error. We want to return to Jesus' identity and authority, characterized here, first by his power manifestations and then by his teaching, which through the story *reads* us, and points us to key understandings and observations concerning what is true and how to live that truth today.

7:24 – 8:21

As the story moves on in 7:24, we read that Jesus departs from where he was in Gennesaret, Jewish territory, to go into the region of Tyre, which again will bring him and his mission, perhaps in a reversal of fortunes, into the Gentile community.

No doubt, as far as narrative construction goes, slotting these next stories into this particular place in the unfolding narrative intends to highlight the growing openness of Jesus to the Gentiles in the face of increasing Jewish opposition and the numerous misunderstandings of the disciples. Frequently, in the Markan narrative, we find Jesus seeking shelter and attempting to avoid the growing crowds. In this context, in the region of Tyre, he aims to escape notoriety, but alas is unsuccessful as word of his reputation had by this time spread through the countryside, as we have been told already back in chapter 3:8.

Immediately, hearing about him being there, no doubt an affirmation of his increasing attraction, and inability to keep the knowledge of his presence quiet, a woman comes to Jesus and falls at his feet because her little daughter has an unclean spirit. She begs Jesus to cast it out. Remember to keep in mind, as the story emphasizes; this is a Gentile woman who has a daughter with an unclean spirit. The racial and ritual risk for Jesus is both dramatic and striking, as the traditional Jewish understanding of cleanliness would have read "astronomically unclean" all over this woman.

Raising the stakes, at this stage of the story, enhances the picture of Jesus as a perceptive and wise boundary crosser. Artificial boundaries proliferated in Jesus' context, much as they do in many Christian circles today, yet Jesus is out to circumvent and dismantle these kinds of human boundaries that blocked the revelation of God from getting through to those who would listen and hear.

Recall that earlier in this narrative we have read about Jesus eating with sinners, healing in synagogues, touching lepers, being touched by a bleeding woman, and reversing understandings of defilement. Jesus, therefore, is crossing boundaries in shocking yet appropriate ways, to create and allow for new dimensions of seeing something of what God was doing now that his kingdom had arrived.

Back in our immediate context of chapter 7, Jesus' response to the Syro-Phoenician woman and her request may strike readers as somewhat mysterious, though in the story the woman is far from mesmerized and she seems to have a valid and fitting comment in return.

What takes place may go something like this. Jesus is reluctant to respond to this request right away. He has come to Tyre for a short rest before further mission activity. He appeals to a cultural perspective that the household children should be satisfied first, as they have priority over dogs, and Jesus may have in mind dogs that live outdoors and scavenge around for food. The woman implicitly agrees with the first point – indeed, she shares this cultural standpoint about children. Yet, she alludes to indoor or pet dogs under the table that feed off the crumbs of children. Jesus' hesitation to act immediately is reversed. Because of this Gentile woman taking his saying and cleverly turning it to her advantage, he grants her request on the spot and the exorcism is accomplished at a distance. Boundary crossings continue with the Gentile woman, and her daughter and Jesus' incredible power is again emphasized.

He then moves on deeper into the Gentile community and healing of a deaf-mute. People implore Jesus on the man's behalf, and he readily responds. Going further than simply placing his hands on the man, Jesus pulls him aside in order fully to concentrate on the man's severe debilitation. Fingers in ears, saliva on the tongue, groaning, and looking heavenward, all emphasizing the extraordinary complexity, Jesus then proclaims, "Be opened" and immediately the man is healed; he both hears and speaks plainly. This spectacular manifestation of power is both bold and emphatic, yet the following picture, as so often, portrays Jesus ordering the people to keep it quiet, though astonishment at what had taken place leads to the contrary. Jesus' futile attempts at quieting reports like this may have been aimed to reduce the already high levels of public speculation about who he was until the time came for further clarification.

The closing comment of chapter 7 affirms Jesus' growing prominence, and perhaps in spite of not an altogether welcoming reputation in Jewish eyes, the Gentile community is utterly astounded – he was one who did everything well and healed even those with the most complex problems and disabilities.

The previous exorcism and healing now open onto further border crossing and another manifestation of power in the Gentile community. While the feeding of four thousand people closely parallels the previous feeding of five thousand, it is important to remember that in the unfolding mission of Jesus these people are, for the most part, not Jewish. Jesus has ventured into the Gentile community and encountered a positive welcome. What remains, before leaving again, is to reduplicate, in some fashion, his powerful feeding of the Jewish people that has already taken place back in chapter 6. Not only does Jesus cross boundaries here with exorcisms and healings, but he powerfully feeds thousands of non-Jews.

The remarkable compassion and power of Jesus are again highlighted. The question of the disciples sets this up nicely, and the little food they have multiplies so that everyone eats to the full and is satisfied, while there is once more, as in the previous feeding of Jews, enough to be collected as leftovers. Without further ado, Jesus, having sent the people away, goes off with the disciples in a boat into another region, which remains somewhat topographically mysterious, even today.

At any rate, the next verses indicate that Jesus and the disciples have arrived back in Jewish territory. The previous welcome in the Gentile community is now abruptly contrasted by a dispute with the Pharisees. Notice these Pharisees are not really wanting dialogue or to ask questions, but rather are deliberately setting up a test.

The encoding of the Pharisees here as phony debaters and dubious questioners aims to alert readers to their real status. They are hostile towards Jesus and do not come seeking to find out more, as they are out to show that he is a charlatan who does not deserve the attention he is receiving.

These Pharisees demand that Jesus give them a sign. What they want though is not a power manifestation – these Jesus had already performed in both Jewish and non-Jewish contexts – what they are insisting on is an authenticating proof that will result in removing the need for faith.

I suppose this may be another of those contexts where we can tend to imitate Pharisees. In similar ways to them asking Jesus for a sign, we do this with God. I have heard this many times, "if God does not give me a sign" and then it even gets much more specific than these Pharisees, "that he will provide for me in this particular way;" a husband or wife, where to live, etc., and if this sign does not materialize "then God must not be God." Such demands and their expected results lack credibility because they put the demander in the wrong position. That is, to require that God give proving signs means that we are attempting to force God to measure up to our specific expectations and if God does not, note the attempted blackmail, we refuse to believe God is God.

There is no problem with making our requests known to God, but when we demand that they be met as signs, or when we base our faith on getting what we demand, we move in the wrong direction. Our testing of God may be similar to the Pharisees' testing of Jesus. If God does not come through with expected goods, then we suppose God is not God. This type of inauthenticity is connected to a drastic misunderstanding of both who God is and who we are. In the variety of ways that we come across of being a false self, this tops the charts.

Jesus, back in the story, begins his response to the sign demanders with an emotive groaning in his spirit and then poses a question about a whole generation that goes unanswered, yet the outcome is that no sign will be given to it. This refusal to respond to what was demanded by the Pharisees comes to a rather abrupt closure. Jesus is out of there, leaving the Pharisees to discern for themselves his rather enigmatic saying.

On their way, in the boat, the disciples and Jesus have some moments together without the Pharisees or crowds. In a rather mundane fashion the narrator - the storyteller - recounts that the disciples had forgotten the loaves of bread and had only one in the boat with them. This statement leads to a remarkably provocative warning by Jesus. Be careful of the leaven-yeast of the Pharisees and Herod. The narrator is not concerned with mapping this out at this point and simply relies on the reader to have made the connection between what has been previously said about Jesus' enemies, and the present warning to the disciples.

Since the disciples, in response to Jesus' warning, are still focused on bread, he sets out to raise other questions in line with the disciples' discussion that will get to the heart of some rather important issues. Thus, Jesus poses several questions that, as we have seen previously, portray the disciples as those who are just not getting it. After what has taken place so far in the story, especially with the two massive feedings, the disciples should not have been worried about a lack of bread. Their continual failure to understand puts them at risk. They are close to those referred to in this gospel as "outsiders" who do not see or hear the present mission of Jesus as the in-breaking KOG in new and fresh ways. For all this time spent with Jesus, the disciples still do not realize who he is and what his mission is out to accomplish. Ironically, those who were presently the enemies of Jesus will in the future be those of the disciples.

Jesus' boundary crossings are crucial for us to remember. Supposed outsiders can be welcomed in and receive his response to their needs. Equally, it is important to keep in mind that his enemies can be outsiders. We too need to "watch out" for the Pharisees and Herod like figures of our times, as we seek to understand better Jesus and the in-breaking KOG.

8:22 – 9:1

The next piece of the story moves us closer to Jerusalem, Jesus' final destination. The heightening drama continues in his mission, and his role of teaching the disciples comes more clearly into focus from here on in the narrative. We recall from last time that Jesus and the disciples have been traveling – back in Jewish territory in this first scene they arrive at Bethsaida. Remember, Jesus, has been showing, in both Jewish and non-Jewish contexts, the in breaking power of the KOG in his person, mission, and teaching.

A blind man is now brought to Jesus for healing. The man is led out of the area, and Jesus spits on his eyes, touches him with his hands and asks him if he can now see anything. The man who is blind responds that he sees something, but not yet clearly. Jesus then touches his eyes, and the man's sight is completely renewed. After he sees, the blind man is sent home and instructed not to go into the village. It is likely that the man does not live in the village and that he came to Jesus from elsewhere. At any rate, Jesus has performed another power manifestation back in Jewish territory, which enables a person to regain sight and then to return home. This is the ninth specific healing so far in the gospel. On the way to Jerusalem only two more will be performed, while remarkably, once Jesus arrives there, no further healings will take place. Evidently, Jesus' journey to Jerusalem is for other reasons, which will fully unfold later.

Following this healing, Jesus and the disciples go into villages around Caesarea Philippi. On the road, Jesus asks them, "Who do the people say I am?" The response takes us back to chapter 6, as the suggestions here seem to reflect on what was proposed as possibilities there. The major question for the disciples and the one we ultimately have to face comes next – Jesus asks, "Who do you say I am?" Of course, this very question has often bewildered them. As we have seen a number of times in the story, they fail to understand Jesus' identity and mission. Peter, likely the spokesman for the group, responds, "You are the Christ – Messiah." Then the narrator adds, "Jesus warned them not to tell anyone about him."

Despite the truth of the reference to the identity of Jesus, he authoritatively orders the disciples to keep this quiet. We might surmise that this another strange command, once Peter and the disciples seem to get it right, but further public speculation about Jesus' identity would have increased unwanted messianic fervor and misunderstanding; as, in just a minute, the following verses will show, albeit within the inner circle of his disciples.

The narrator opens the next scene with Jesus teaching about the Son of Man. This self-identifying way he often referred to himself shows the purposeful shift from Messiah to a self-reference with greater ambiguity, at this particular stage in the story. This is a necessary move to begin to refigure current understandings of Messiah, especially in the lives of Peter and the disciples and any who are to follow Jesus.

The Son of Man will suffer and face the rejection of the Jewish religious elite in Jerusalem, be killed by a corrupt political system, and then after three days be raised. Just then Peter, again likely to be highlighted as the spokesman for the disciples, calls Jesus' portrayal of himself into question. Peter challenges him. No doubt the disciples would be shocked by this dire prediction, in spite of the notion of "rising again" and Peter boldly rebukes Jesus for such apparent folly. Perhaps, one of the most difficult things to accept is that Jesus may not be comfortably situated in human perceptions of any current messianic ideology. Imaginary constructs and unrealistic hopes, as in Peter's case, can often also turn us into our own Messiah makers. Messiah making is a risky and dangerous enterprise and something we all tend to do in one way or the other.

Notice the turn of Jesus to his disciples in verse 33 is a subtle, yet forceful indication that Peter is in the wrong place. His ideology and pseudo-stature betray him. His need is to return to his place as a follower, rather than to presume a capacity of equality that goes far beyond his own, hence Jesus' strong words of comparison with Peter and the enemy who opposes the things of God. In Peter's case, he is following his own tradition characterized here as "the things of men." Unfortunately, this is something we all can frequently do.

Peter and the disciples seem to be caught up in a messianic ideology that Jesus is now out to reverse and reformulate. Their views need to undergo shock therapy in the context of suffering, rejection, and ultimately the death and rising from the dead, of the Messiah – all of which would have presented them with a deeply disturbing enigma, especially as alluded to in 9:10.

After this Jesus gathers together a crowd of people along with his disciples to offer a fresh insight into the meaning of following him. Triumphant, or other types of messianic ideologies, will have to be significantly modified or even let go of altogether.

To come after Jesus first means to deny oneself. This does not mean to become a zero, but it is to put our self-centered interests aside, especially with regard to messianic ideology, and to embrace another, namely God and then the things of God. Doing so is to be cross taking and following in the footsteps of Jesus. Self-denial then is denying a particular picture of self – a self-consumed self – a self-centered self – a self-sufficient self - a messiah making self – a selfish self – a false self. Taking one's cross and following Jesus will result in appropriate self-denial, versus what we often see in our contemporary context that imposes upon people the ridiculous notion that they are somehow to wipe out the totality of who they are so that God can take complete control of their lives. Such notions amount to following the traditions of humans, not the things of God. Jesus next turns to affirm that any who aim to save their life will lose it because they do not deny self, take a cross, and follow Jesus, but if any do lose life for his sake and the gospel, it will be saved.

Even though there is a potential risk of losing life now, Jesus assumes those who decide to come after him will save their lives in doing so. Similarly, gaining the whole world, expressed in all the trappings of the present life, is hardly worth what it portrays at face value. Every self-means so much more than this and therefore would lose in the deal. No possession, achievement or recognition in this world merits following oneself and any messiah making ideology connected to this.

Jesus' further proclamation here is prefaced by the authoritative, "Amen, I say to you." He promises that some with him will not die, prior to being aware that the KOG has come with power – a direct relation to the portrayal of the Daniel 7 figure, with which he identifies himself. There could be several explanations for what such a witnessing might entail, ranging from the following: transfiguration, resurrection, or ascension of Jesus, the outpouring of the Spirit, to the fall of Jerusalem in AD 70.

In my view, there is no way to be sure here as the saying itself is not concerned with precision, as the KOG coming with power is likely to have multiple referents and expressions.

I believe, at this point, we are probably on safer ground not to promote over-speculation, realizing that the KOG has already come near in Jesus' person, mission, and ministry. He has challenged disciples and crowds to pay attention to God's in-breaking reign in his teaching, healing, and exorcisms; in short, his power manifestations. At any rate, therefore, it seems highly unlikely that this is a declaration about the second coming and we shall have to wait and see how this plays out in what follows.

9:1 – 13

At this point, you may find that you want to refresh or renew a section, or even start again from the beginning of the narrative. Stories are like that – they invite us into their world, but to be able to recognize this world and dwell in it, it is helpful to perceive something of its unfolding. If you have time – re-visit earlier scenes in the story. Parts will begin to fit into wholes, and this imaginatively enables and cultivates new understanding. Before jumping into chapter 9, I'll highlight some of the more salient trajectories so that we will be better equipped, as we approach the rest of the narrative.

In the first chapter of Mark's story, we find John preaching repentance and baptizing in the Jordan. Jesus comes from Nazareth and is baptized – he receives the Spirit and is commended and loved by God, as voiced from heaven. Following his baptism, but before his public mission begins, Jesus is sent out into the desert and tempted by Satan. After John's imprisonment, Jesus goes into Galilee proclaiming the good news of God and that the KOG was near – therefore, repent and believe. He invites Peter and Andrew to follow him and immediately they do.

Jesus' first exhibition of power is casting out an unclean spirit in a synagogue in Capernaum. People are amazed at his teaching and authority, and news of him begins to spread far and wide. Jesus' power manifestations multiply – he performs three specific healings, calls more disciples to follow him and responds to questions from the teachers of the law and the Pharisees. And then the crowds are often with Jesus wherever he goes. They are astonished by his acts of power and his new and radical teaching.

Moving further into Mark's narrative, Jesus continues exhibiting his power through healing, appoints the twelve disciples, fends off family concerns about his sanity, and faces accusations that he is casting out demons by Beelzebub. The culmination of these incidents is Jesus' controversial remark that his true family is made up of those who do God's will, thereby undermining the typically strong blood familial ties of his culture.

Next, the narrator gives a series of Jesus' teaching in parables, followed by his first natural-spiritual power manifestation, leaving the disciples terrified and asking, "Who is this?" an ongoing question throughout the narrative.

In chapter 5 we read about another exorcism, one that leaves the crowds utterly amazed. This is quickly followed by two further specific healings, which gives a partial response to the disciples' previous question. Yet in Nazareth, his hometown, people take offense at him.

At this point, Jesus sends out the twelve on a preliminary mission to take authority over unclean spirits. The narrator follows this sending out with the gruesome story of the beheading of John the Baptist – conveying to the reader the chilling presence of opposition and highlighting Jesus' growing popularity as his public and political presence has even caught King Herod's attention.

Jesus then feeds five thousand people in Jewish territory. He performs another natural-spiritual miracle, debates with the Pharisees about what makes a person clean and unclean, and teaches the disciples it is what is inside that counts. Following this teaching, we read of two more specific healings and then the account of Jesus feeding four thousand people in non-Jewish territory; the disciples accompany him and collect the leftovers from the abundance of food.

Chapter 8 offers an explicit picture of the disciples' failure to understand who Jesus is, amounting to Jesus posing a direct question to them: "Who do you say that I am?" Peter's response – "You are the Christ" – is theoretically correct, however, after Jesus' first prediction of his death, it seems that Peter and the disciples have a different idea of who "the Christ" is.

Now with these trajectories in mind, we are better equipped to dig into chapter nine, beginning with a somewhat bewildering comment from Jesus in 9:1.

There are many things to bear in mind while reading this passage. Peter and the disciples' true, but misunderstood response to Jesus' question; Jesus' first prediction of his death; his rebuke of Peter; the concept of losing life in order to find it; and the arrival of the Son of Man. With these details before us, we can better understand Jesus' remark as a further attempt to clarify who he is and what his mission ultimately entails.

As an assurance in the face of his imminent death and for those following him, Jesus declares that there will be some who will not die until they see the KOG come in power. There are several possible referents for such a manifestation, including Jesus' death and resurrection, the ascension and outpouring of the Spirit, and the fall of Jerusalem in AD 70. At any rate, precision is not required as there was to be a diversity of ways for this assurance to be perceived and realized. The next scene is a powerful example of at least a partial fulfillment of Jesus' comment.

Normally in Mark's narrative, time sequences are not specified, and many things take place 'immediately' or 'at once.' The lapse of six days here may serve to connect the coming event with verse 1 and to account for a time of preparation, perhaps echoing Moses' and Elijah's encounters with God on Mount Sinai.

Taking three disciples, Jesus leads the way up a high mountain. He is then transfigured before them – undergoing a metamorphosis, a startling change. Not only does he change, but his clothes glisten with a spiritual quality that supposes the more familiar, but perhaps now ephemeral, shades of white. This extraordinary theophany includes the appearance of the OT figures of Elijah and Moses, both of whom experienced mountain theophanies, although this time it is Jesus who is fulfilling and assuring the stunned disciples. Moses and Elijah were OT forerunners of the

Messiah, both known in Judaism as high profile characters looking forward to an end time figure who would fulfill and go beyond any role either had performed in leading the people of God.

The presence of Moses and Elijah interacting with the transfigured Jesus provokes Peter to fearfully suggest that the disciples' value in being present is to build three shelters for the three other-worldly persons amongst them. Undoubtedly, one can relate to their fear and need for a purpose during such a mesmerizing encounter – in highly precarious situations one is prone to attempt to underline the value of her/his presence to those who hold her/his fate in their hands.

At this moment, a cloud appears shrouding them all – now we can imagine the disciples' level of terror increasing a level or two – and then a voice booms through the mist. Clouds are often associated with theophanies in the OT, particularly when God speaks to Moses in Exodus on several occasions. The pronouncement, "This is my Son whom I love. Listen to him!" marks the authenticity of Jesus as Messiah – he who knew the way forward in spite of the inappropriate and misunderstood Messiah making on the disciples' behalf. With this remarkable affirmation of Jesus' sonship, these disciples have witnessed something of the KOG coming with power, although there remains much more to come.

In the next instant, the disciples are shielding their eyes, then they look around, and everything had changed; they again find themselves alone with the Son of Man, yet with he who is also the beloved Son of God, to whom they have been charged to listen.

During their descent from the mountaintop experience, Jesus instructs them – no doubt to avoid further misinterpretation and misunderstanding about his Messiahship – not to tell anyone about their experience until the Son of Man has risen from the dead. The narrator confirms that this was what took place, adding that Jesus' statement about the resurrection bewildered the disciples.

While resurrection would not have been entirely mysterious in those times, it was a notion that would have required clarification as to date, time, and place. For Jesus to speak of his resurrection within the context of history is likely to have brought a fresh perspective, especially with regard to the long-awaited Messiah, who on most accounts was an anticipated kingly figure coming with power on the last day to restore justice for the people of God, namely, the Jews. A Messiah who would first be killed to then be resurrected would take some refiguring in the disciples' hearts and minds.

The combination of the transfiguration, the voice from the cloud, Moses' and Elijah's presence, and Jesus' mention of resurrection prompt the disciples to question the timing of the coming Messiah. Following scribal tradition, which may have relied on Malachi, the last book of the OT, the disciples want to know where things are concerning the unfolding arrival of the KOG.

Elijah was expected to precede and announce the day of the Lord before the Messiah arrived – he was the eschatological marker that scribes assumed would map out the last days. Jesus' response confirms, yet modifies the scribes' teaching. Elijah's mission in Malachi 4 is to restore Israel's wayward paths and to prepare the people for a Divine visitation. Yet then, Jesus asks, why or how can it be written that the Son of Man may suffer much and be treated with contempt? Jesus' question effectively shifts the disciples' question from Elijah coming to his own imminent suffering and rejection.

By posing this rhetorical query, he aims to highlight that the time of restoration has to be considered from another angle. Jesus then stresses that Elijah, instead of still having to come, has already arrived. That is, Elijah has returned, typologically speaking, in the person of John the Baptist who called the people to repentance, yet as we have read back in chapter 6, was imprisoned and beheaded. What the enemies of Elijah attempt to do to him in the days of 1 Kings 17-19, although unsuccessful, has now taken place. This then is not the time of restoration, but a time of suffering, injustice, and brutal rejection that both Elijah, John, and the Son of Man – Jesus – have to go through before that final day comes. In closing, we might say that Jesus' transfiguration opens the way for a new Exodus in that the disciples of Jesus are invited to see the KOG come with power, yet this manifestation is one of others to follow.

The voice from heaven is an assurance that Jesus is God's loved Son. Listen to him. Messiah making of our own, whatever form it takes, is *utterly* inappropriate. As John before him, Jesus will suffer and be rejected, yet the day of final restoration and the close of history has not arrived, although there will be further manifestations in the narrative that this day will indeed come.

9:14 – 50

Following the transfiguration of Jesus and the three disciples' witness to something of the KOG coming in power, they all now rejoin the other disciples who are in the midst of a controversy with the scribes.

At this point, the crowd, becoming aware of Jesus' arrival on the scene, is astonished that he, not merely his disciples, is now present. His magnetism draws the crowd to him, and the narrator highlights this attraction. Jesus then wants to know what the dispute is all about. Intriguingly, on the story level, neither the scribes nor the disciples respond. The man in the crowd who must have precipitated the controversy now answers Jesus' question. He politely and respectfully states: "Teacher, I brought my son to you" (and then by implication, hoping you would be available, but this was not the case), "because my son is mute spirit possessed, which affects his speech." His son, note, is also dominated by this spirit in other destructive ways. While the boy's condition might have some medical explanation, the story here maintains that there is more at stake. The inability of the disciples to meet the father's request now comes to the surface. Originally, looking for Jesus to help, the father found his disciples, who don't have the strength to cast out the spirit.

Jesus then expresses his frustration concerning the whole scenario, where "unbelieving generation" probably includes all those involved in the dispute and the gravity of their unbelief, expressed in Jesus' emotive questions. "How long shall I be with you? How long shall I put up with you?" Seeking to address this unbelief and the plight of the possessed boy, Jesus turns to a power manifestation to make his point.

Once the boy is brought to him the spirit immediately reacts in violent physical convulsions; the narrator is stressing here the power of the spirit over the boy. The following question and answer concerning, "How long?" and "from childhood" highlight that this problem is one of long duration; hence the severity of the boy's condition, which the father's further remark only serves to underscore. The task before Jesus is monumental, and so much so that the father remains on the grounds of the disciples' failure, somewhat unsure about Jesus' ability to make any substantial difference. "Nevertheless" the father states, "if you are able any help would be of value."

Jesus, picking up on this comment, raises another question that goes something like, "If you are able?" and then responds well, in fact, all things can be done for the person who believes. At once the father proclaims that he believes, yet most likely because of the disciples' failure to cast out the spirit, there remains a residue of unbelief. Notice that the father's attitude, as recounted here, is not one that dwells on unbelief, but one that requests the help of Jesus to overcome it.

Now, with all this in place the exorcism can be performed – for the boy, the father, the disciples, the crowd and Jesus himself – as his credibility and power are on the line. With the crowd surging in upon them, Jesus chooses this moment to challenge, what is now referred to as, the unclean spirit, and powerfully command it to come out and never enter the boy again. In this confrontation of power Jesus' ability to expel the spirit triumphs and it comes out, leaving the boy with the appearance of being dead – perhaps again emphasizing the powerful effect of this spirit in order to highlight Jesus' greater power and the reality of the exorcism.

As will be the case a number of times in the narrative from here on, the disciples receive teaching about this scenario from Jesus. On this occasion, they learn that prayer is important for their power engagement with unclean spirits. The implication here is that the disciples may have over-estimated their ability to be successful in these types of power encounters and depended too greatly on themselves, rather than on God or their association with Jesus and his power, which seems to have previously been available to them. Thus, the contrast is between them and Jesus. They must pray and rely on powers that are not their own, while Jesus need not necessarily do so. The whole story intends to capture something of the dynamic strength and power of Jesus, yet it remains instructive for his disciples whose growing presence and place in the narrative begins to come more clearly into view. What a remarkable character Jesus was and is, as previously marked out in the story through a significant series of power encounters, although from here on out his teaching will take greater precedence, over his power manifestations.

Jesus, now passing by Galilee, is aiming to remain incognito in order to spend more time teaching the disciples. He returns to predict again, as previously in 8:31, his death and resurrection. This monumental occasion draws ever closer in each step of the journey towards Jerusalem.

One can be somewhat sympathetic to the disciples' lack of understanding. Jesus powerfully casts out unclean spirits, yet his power is incapable of withstanding and overthrowing a plot to kill him. The reason for this will become clear as the narrative unfolds. At this stage, the disciples' fear illuminates the powerful, yet mysterious character of Jesus as the Son of Man, who for the second time predicts his death and resurrection – both apparent enigmas to his fearful followers.

As they arrive in Capernaum, it turns out that on the way the disciples were disputing highly insignificant matters and again need to be taught a new perspective – a new way of perceiving themselves and Jesus. He poses his question in verse 33 seeking to have the disciples open up about their debate, of which Jesus is already aware. This occasion gives rise to a series of important teachings. The aim or goal of following Jesus is not to consider oneself better or more important than the other. Reversing the disciples clamoring to be first, Jesus agrees it is better to be last – better to serve than to master.

Taking a child and embracing him he wants to teach the disciples that those of lowly status – the unimportant, as children were in Jesus' day, are those that are to be invited and received. To do so in Jesus' name; for his sake, is to welcome him, but even more than this, to welcome the One who sent him. Intriguingly, Jesus does not claim final reference for himself, but refers to the sender – to God, and ultimately receiving him through embracing those like children in status. To pursue greatness or being first will repeatedly lack truth and love, which closes out or turns away those like children, and as such, blocks reception of Jesus and the One who sent him. Doing this is to falsify oneself continually.

A related issue now arises concerning status. John's question about someone other than one of the twelve using Jesus' name to cast out demons highlights again the disciples, and in particular John's need for a new perspective. Jesus' view is that this person should not be stopped and he gives three reasons for his command and "in my name" is the key to them all. Doing exorcism in Jesus' name shows enough affiliation and identification in this context to point out that this person will not slander Jesus. While someone like this might be an "outsider," this should not necessarily make the person an enemy. Likewise, when hospitality is offered "in my name" to those who belong to Jesus – another emphasis on "my name," the person showing true signs of faith in the gospel and then performing actions corresponding to it, will not lose a reward.

Outsiders, therefore, who are not explicitly following Jesus around, as the disciples were, does not mean, should they be doing what they're doing "in his name," that their efforts are invalid. His disciples, focused on status and sectarian views of the other, need a new perception, though this is not open to whoever or whatever, but limited to "in my name."

Of course, this kind of proposal may raise questions for us today – we might think – well, lots of people say this "in my name," but does it really amount to much when there is apparently a deep lack of correspondence between saying and doing? Or, on the other hand, we may observe lots of doing, but little saying. There are simply no certain fail-safe guarantees here. We must aim to have an appropriate configuration of trust and suspicion – first towards ourselves and then with respect to the other – recognizing that this dynamic will not be static, but in motion finding a direction where "in my name" resonates with a saying and doing that corresponds – not perfectly; but lovingly and redemptively, to the Messiah.

In contrast, now in verse 42, to the previous person, doing things "in Jesus' name," this person is severely warned to be careful about the treatment of those who believe in Jesus. Causing one of these to stumble or trip – to fall down or away from faith will be counted an extremely serious offense.

Jesus returns to the disciples in particular and in verse 43 targets the problematic; not of the other, but of oneself. All these sayings refer to *body* parts to make the point about the seriousness of a variety of perspectives that may cause sin. (You will notice that verses 44 and 46 do not appear in most translations. This is because they repeat verse 48 and are not found in the earliest or best manuscripts).

Jesus strongly stresses the dynamic of a hermeneutics of trust and suspicion. A necessary ingredient of perceiving sin in one's life is to be suspicious and not merely trust one's thoughts, feelings, or actions as Godly. On the other hand, foot, or eye, trusting oneself is a requirement for being suspicious – therefore trust and suspicion have to incorporate a Godly dimension to function in a life-giving manner.

Volumes have been written on verse 48 and the contrasts of the three previous occasions, between life and hell. Suffice it to say that life is the destiny of a follower of Jesus – shall we say, a mode of being present with God in a lasting way, whereas "hell" (gehenna) is frequently a term found in apocalyptic sayings – referring to a place for the dead bodies of the ungodly, notably a garbage dump outside Jerusalem – the picture here is borrowed from Isaiah 66:24. Precisely how this saying is to be interpreted remains a matter of debate and caution may be closest to wisdom when it comes to such graphic imagery of deterrence similar to the preceding verses. At any rate, many serious dangers face disciples of Jesus, and each follower is to practice shockingly investigative and evaluative measures to identify sin and take radical action against it.

Concluding this series of teachings, the narrator adds – not only disciples as previously, but everyone will find themselves in a position of accountability. This salt and fire imagery may also apply more narrowly to disciples. That is, followers of Jesus may experience life-risking sacrificial contexts, as in times of old, where salt was included in giving offerings to God.

A surplus of meaning, therefore, highlights the use of salt as something beneficial – Jesus seems to be alluding to the relevance of disciples being salty ones. Their demands for greatness, excluding outsiders, ignoring those of little status, or engaging in other sinful practices, will result in becoming unsalty. And thus they will not be accomplishing the purpose salt is used for as a preservative of being at peace with each other, instead of disputing over matters of little significance compared to what it really means to follow in the footsteps of Jesus and to embrace his new perspectives, while being challenged by the radical vision he offers.

10:1 – 52

We see a familiar picture at the outset of chapter 10. Jesus is now again in the midst of teaching crowds of people. On this occasion, as he travels towards his terrible destiny in Jerusalem, the Pharisees put him to the test. They are interested in trying to trip Jesus up over the subject of divorce. On a reading of Deuteronomy 24:1-4 many Jewish men in Jesus' day practiced easy divorce. Burning dinner, for example, could have given sufficient cause for a man to put aside his wife and marry someone else.

Jesus, as often, responds to the Pharisees' question with his own. They provocatively ask is it lawful for a man to divorce his wife? He counters – what did Moses command? They respond from Deuteronomy 24 suggesting that Moses permitted, note not commanded divorce.

The part of the Torah the Pharisees have in mind, Jesus points out, was a concession to hard hearts. He prefers another possibility referencing bits of the two stories of beginnings in Genesis 1 and 2. From the perspective of beginnings in the creation stories, Jesus says, in so many words: marriage is intended to be permanent, as God has something to do with the two becoming one flesh. On these grounds, divorce is wrong, although we would suggest that in some situations it may be necessary, which is not dealt with here.

The scene quickly changes without giving readers any idea of what these Pharisees thought of Jesus' perspective. Now in the house, the disciples query his meaning. Based on a widespread Jewish presupposition that divorce was often an excuse to remarry, Jesus picks up the implication of this common understanding.

His view, however, goes strongly against the cultural norm and the misinterpretation of Deuteronomy 24, stating that remarriage is adultery, be it from man's initiative in a Jewish context, where women did not have this option to divorce or from the woman's initiative in the Greco-Roman context, where they did. Verses 10-12, more specifically, affirm that divorce for remarriage is wrong. Considering these complex personal matters, it is best to keep in mind the values and perspectives of Jesus' teaching on love and forgiveness found elsewhere in other contexts. This will not change his perspective on divorce being wrong, but it will highlight the need to be sensitive and constructive.

Be it divorce or remarriage – the relational reality holds – normally, at least in Jesus' teaching here, as opposed to Jewish and Roman perspectives; divorce is wrong and remarriage after divorce would be adultery. Notice nothing is said here about those being divorced and their situation – again, this shows, I believe, that we need to consider Jesus' strong statements in this context and then how other parts of his teaching would come to bear on these extremely difficult issues.

With the focus now on continuing to teach the disciples, the next part of the story pulls us back in the direction of highlighting the need for followers of Jesus to have a new perspective, and this time it concerns children. This scene reminds us of the questions of the status of children that were already raised back in chapter 9. Here we are given another portrayal of the KOG. Parents are bringing their children to Jesus, and for some reason, the disciples find this problematic. Jesus points out that those who adopt an attitude of a child-like status, at least in this cultural perspective, where children were not the center of attention as they often are today, understand the importance of humility over arrogance and receiving over possessing. The KOG not only belongs to these, but it must be received and accepted in trust to be entered.

Another important issue abruptly arises next in verses 17-31. A man runs towards Jesus and kneels before him, seemingly having some understanding of who he is. This spontaneous, even excessive behavior, may underline the seriousness of the man's quest to have a definitive answer or at least affirmation of this current status and destiny.

Jesus responds to the man's address, "Good teacher," with – "no one is good, but one – God alone." This response may subtly, yet radically present a double irony. First, Jesus claims God alone is good – a shocking proclamation, especially to Jewish ears – but his question, "Why do you call me good?" – may, in fact, be an affirmation that he is good. Second, in going further in the story in just a minute, it becomes clear that the man saw himself as good and therefore Jesus wants to open up the possibility that he should be more suspicious of his own evaluations concerning his status.

Next, the man's question about what to do to live forever receives attention. Jesus assumes this man knows his Decalogue and lists several behavior attitudes and actions towards others as an initial and perhaps probing response. After hearing these, the man comes back with "Teacher" (dropping the good, likely because he misses Jesus' subtle self-identification with "good,") and then says, "Since my youth, my behavior concerning these commands has been exemplary."

Then, Jesus looks intensely at him. We can imagine this is not so much with suspicion, but trust, and loves him. Perhaps, Jesus is touched by this man's audacity, reverence, sincerity, and willingness to follow God's commands. What this man is lacking, however, Jesus responds, is that which is truly necessary – to sell what he has, and give to the poor in order to have a different sort of treasure in heaven – this is a forever life – and then, Jesus adds, come and follow me. The invitation requires the double price of letting go of earthly possessions and letting go of an identity that is shaped and captured by them, and in exchange having an everlasting life.

This suggestion of a reversal of fortunes saddens the man, and he frowns in consternation and departs. In anticipating the disciples' bewilderment, Jesus comments further about the difficulty of a rich person entering the KOG, as exemplified in the interaction which has just taken place. The disciples' reaction to this now turns from bewilderment to surprise – Jesus again intervenes addressing them with something like "Listen, as I said – how hard it is to enter the KOG," probably still implying a rich person, as the next saying illustrates. What was difficult previously is now, with the picture of a camel going through the eye of a needle, impossible.

At this stage of the proceedings, the disciples are about to bail out. They're stunned. Discouraged, they wonder – then who can be saved? Or preserved? Or live a lasting life? Perhaps, they are thinking about the rich and now needed a new perspective, albeit one that is not spelled out with precision as Jesus' following remark illustrates. What is impossible for humans is not for God because all things are possible with God. But here again, as we have previously seen in this story, Jesus does not articulate exactly how this applies and it is somewhat left up to the reader to work it out on the basis of the reality of their own context in light of Jesus' overall teaching.

It seems to me that we should neither ignore the human problem of possessions and how they might make it impossible for one to enter the KOG, nor should we insist that the human perspective is all that matters for the entry of a rich person. Possessive attitudes to possessions will render entry impossible – but this is not the end of the story. I would think that our trajectory here has to be similar to the one we marked out in previous scenarios. That is, sometimes our longings, or even demands for black and white will have to be replaced by that which we've been given and then we have to do our very best with what we have. This means that we have to be willing to explore Jesus' teachings a bit more holistically in order to have a broader perspective that will hopefully help us, yet may not make everything crystal clear.

At this point, Peter interjects on behalf of the disciples and stresses that they, in contrast to the rich man, have left all and followed Jesus. Perhaps, it might give some perspective here to recall that Peter continued to have a house, which Jesus had been in, and probably a fishing boat or two, along with a selection of nets. Peter and the other disciples had indeed left behind some people and possessions for this particular time to accompany Jesus, and being invited to follow him and therefore became fishers of others. And this may at least partially explain, we'll see in just a moment, why the third prediction that Jesus makes of his death and resurrection is situated right after his closing words on this controversial issue. That is, following Jesus geographically on the ground, is for a limited period and yes, yes, of course, is a sacrifice in the present context of discipleship. Jesus though now goes on to address, it seems, both geographical following related to his present disciples, and non-geographical following for all disciples post-resurrection.

Jesus stresses that no one has left relations or possessions for him and the good news, who won't receive hundred times as much of the same in the present, and the age to come, but likely not in a literal sense. The hundred times as much might, in fact, come from one person, or a whole extended family, or more broadly a community or church that offers shelter, hospitality, love and challenging grace, which can and does fill life far beyond that which the rich man returned to in consternation. But notice this is not all in store for the disciple because, with this gain, there will also be a loss, or to say it otherwise, persecution.

Jesus closes out this story with another reversal. The new perspective for disciples is that they should not assume some inordinate superiority, but be aware that the entering into the KOG is not set up for those who demand to be first in line, acknowledging the reality that to be last in this *economy* is really to be first. As already mentioned, Jesus' third prediction of his death and resurrection now follows, but it is reserved for the twelve amidst a group of travelers on the way to Jerusalem.

Following Jesus' prediction in the narrative, we have two brothers coming to him. You will recall, they witnessed, along with Peter, the transfiguration, and now would like Jesus to do what they ask. It seems like they may have the previous hundred times benefit in the present and age to come in mind. There are only two possibilities in this scenario; right and left. Their fellow disciple, Peter, and the others remain excluded.

Does blood run thicker than discipleship? And being first over last? Jesus, the suspicious fellow that he is, wants to know, before responding, what it is these brothers want. And, here it is – each wants a position or status in his glory. But Jesus responds that they aren't aware of what they're asking. While they might drink the cup and be baptized with his baptism, it is not his place to decide the configuration of those to be nearest to him. Such places in all likelihood are prepared by God.

The narrator alerts us next to the anger of the other disciples concerning the request of the brothers. Jesus then pulls them together and repeats the new perspective he has been putting forward on the last couple of teaching occasions. He continues to reverse roles, underlining that serving is the way of true discipleship. Jesus' self-reference in verse 45, along with its evident allusions to Isaiah 53 and the suffering servant so prominent there, marks out his mission here. Service and giving his life as a ransom for the release of many – the former is the key to confessing and following Jesus, while the latter belongs to him alone.

The story now winds its way to Jericho and recounts the eleventh and last specific healing, which takes place just before entering Jerusalem. This healing, another remarkable power manifestation of Jesus has the effect of mirroring back to 8:22-26 and the ninth healing, which also was of a blind man, but there at the outset of the journey towards Jerusalem.

Bartimaeus, a blind beggar, hearing that Jesus of Nazareth, not just a person named Jesus, was passing by shouts into the crowd, "Jesus, Son of

David have mercy on me." The narrator doesn't mention this, but perhaps because Bartimaeus begged on the side of the road on the way to Jerusalem, he heard lots of stories about the healing powers of Jesus of Nazareth, and Son of David. The latter is a Messianic echo, just before the Jerusalem entry; so he is not shouting without hope, and he keeps doing so in spite of those who seek to silence him.

The only person named in all of Jesus' healings is Bartimaeus, perhaps because of his insight and audacity. He is now called by Jesus and asked what he wants. "Rabbi," he says, "I want to see." Jesus grants, on the basis of Bartimaeus' faith, his request to see through yet another power manifestation, and at once Bartimaeus receives his sight and is now free to go and follow Jesus on the way to Jerusalem.

From chapter 8:22 and the healing of a blind man at Bethsaida to 10:46 and the healing of Bartimaeus just before the imminent entry into Jerusalem, we have seen that Jesus' power manifestations diminish, while the teaching of new perspectives to his disciples increases. No less than three times only in this part of the story Jesus predicts, much to the disciples' bewilderment, that he will be a dead and risen Messiah.

11:1 – 33

And with that in place, we are now ready to enter Jerusalem. In the next stage of Jesus' journey towards death and resurrection, he will enter Jerusalem where no healings or exorcisms will take place. He will face serious opposition here, albeit after experiencing a jubilant welcome. At any rate, Jesus is now out to publicly demonstrate his identity – the time has come for a further unveiling of his character and plans.

The first thing Jesus does is to instruct two disciples to go and fetch an unridden donkey, to untie it, and bring it to him. This looks like a fairly well-planned maneuver, as attested to in Jesus' remarks to his disciples and the disciples' response. It would seem Jesus has sorted the details out and with the assurance that the Lord needs and will return the donkey there will be no objection when the disciples arrive to untie it and take it with them.

Once they return to Jesus with the donkey and lay their cloaks over it, Jesus can be the first to ride it, in keeping with his mastery and now presenting himself as a Messianic figure entering what is thought to be the holy city of Jerusalem.

Crowds pay homage to Jesus, spreading garments and branches on the road, perhaps the distance of a couple of kilometers, implying honor and marking a celebration. There are shouts of "Hosanna" and affirmations of blessing and the coming of the kingdom of David, echoing Psalm 118: 25-26. After this magnificent expression of Jesus' Messiahship, when he enters Jerusalem he goes to check out the temple in order to plan his strategy for the next day. As it is late, Jesus and the twelve retreat to Bethany.

Next, we see another example of the narrative strategy of interpolation. That is, we recall, inserting one story in another so that the reader benefits from how the two incidents or scenes interpret and play off each other. Notice how the temple story that begins in verse 11 and the story of the fig tree in verse 12 are combined and with the rare mention, at least in Mark's narrative, of the time sequences to these stories.

The next day Jesus and the disciples are on their way back to Jerusalem. Jesus, getting hungry, sees a fig tree in leaf some distance away and he goes to it looking for something to eat, but on arrival finds only inedible leaves, with the narrator adding, "because it was not the time for figs." Whether it was too early or too late to find something to eat on the tree is a matter of conjecture, but considering the appearance of it being full of leaves, Jesus still found nothing to eat. He then pronounces to the tree - "May no one eat fruit from you again" with the narrator adding "and his disciples heard him," probably looking forward to verse 20. Fig trees carried a fair amount of significance in Israel – notably in at least these two ways: they usually gave plenty of fruit, as Israel was to do toward the world and were sometimes configured as a marker/symbol for the last days.

Now arriving in Jerusalem, Jesus carries out what he had probably planned the day before, driving out those buying and selling in the temple area. It seems as if the real issue here is not so much with the necessary actions of changing money for the temple tax, or animals and other items for sacrifice being available, but with the location in which all this was taking place. Jesus overturns tables of money changers, upsets the dove sellers' seats, and forbids anyone to enter the temple court area with merchandise. He does this not because he is against these activities per se, but because they are taking place where they should not be; that is, in the temple area – a vast space where Jews would now gather to do business, and this threw the possibility of prayer and teaching in this area into chaos.

Jesus does not take kindly to these types of business transactions in the temple area and in his teaching quotes Isaiah 56:7 and Jeremiah 7:11 to make his case from the OT, "My house will be called a house of prayer for all, but you have made it a 'den of robbers'." No doubt such bold appeals would have jolted the senses of those who heard, especially if they had some awareness of the Jeremiah context where the temple itself is predicted to be in danger of destruction.

The chief priests and scribes, notably, are attuned to Jesus' pronouncements and their trajectory, which causes them to want to kill him as he threatens their status. Jesus, they recognize, is a subversive character. He radically rebels against the authorities, calling into question their way of doing things and at this point, the crowd approves of his actions and is amazed at his teaching. Departing from the temple and

Jerusalem opens up to the next morning – again the time sequencing in the story is unusual, but mentioned here to highlight what comes next.

In the withering of the fig tree, we see both the prophetic character of Jesus' previous saying in verse 14 now fulfilled and another striking power manifestation. Peter is the one who recalls Jesus' saying and confirms its result. The curse of the fig tree, as Peter has it, brought it to an end. Since the tree appearing to bear fruit and offering something to eat, did not produce, the curse may carry implications for the temple in Jerusalem, and that is why these stories are recounted together.

Jesus' actions in the temple courts, therefore, may not have been intended merely to cleanse the temple, but even more radically to begin to bring it to an end – to destroy it from its very roots to its leaves. The gesture then looks ahead to chapter 13:1-2 [READ] where Jesus confirms that the temple will be destroyed.

The narrator's purpose in integrating the two stories and the unusual time sequencing connected to them is to pre-figure the coming judgment of God upon Israel for its unfaith. Yet, before the destruction of the temple will be more bluntly announced (as we have seen in chapter 13,) Jesus uses the two stories to teach the disciples and to confront the religious elite.

Our next verses may carry some double innuendos that I will leave to you to reflect on. In verse 22 Jesus pronounces, in response to Peter's remembering and then highlighting the withered fig tree, "Have faith in God." He is stressing his own faith in God and that the disciples' faith is to be in God and what God is doing in Jesus, not themselves or the temple. To let go of faith in the temple with its meta-religious God identification, shocking as it may be, is not to reject faith in God. Jesus implies that the temple is barren, and God is not there, but such a thought would have been entirely subversive for Jesus' hearers.

Jesus' next statement about "this" mountain may pertain to a particular mountain that would have been connected to the Jewish teaching that the house of God in the last days would be built as a fortress on a high mountain. Jesus here, in another way perhaps, is confirming the pending judgment on the temple – the house of God that will be, as it were, proverbially thrown into the sea, traditionally viewed as a place of destruction.

The point is, God's intentions and purposes will come to pass and therefore to believe and not doubt is a real possibility under these circumstances. To speak of something happening and seeing it happen in due recourse invites the mountain thrower to embrace the faithfulness of God in carrying out his intentions, be they regarding the temple, Jesus, or anything else.

The next verse – verse 24, is one of those controversial verses that create a fair amount of confusion. I have puzzled over verses like this, given up on trying to make sense of them, but then returned again to pour over the text, commentaries, and other writings, only be to be left bewildered. But last night, in renewing my efforts, I came up with some thoughts that may shed new light on our understanding. You don't have to agree with my views, but there may be some value in this proposal.

First, it seems to me that when we read verse 24, we tend to do so out of context. This verse needs to fit into the story context of what's going on here, which is centered on the temple. Second, we usually focus on "whatever you ask for" rather than on "in prayer." I want to wager that this former focus is convoluted and creates a myriad of confusion. Third, the terms "in prayer" themselves set a limit on "whatever you ask" because prayer has its referent in God, who has a character and intentions that restrict the domain of asking. One can't ask for anything whatsoever that would not connect with God. Fourth, and more directly related to the disciples, was their limited context of the Jewish temple previously pictured as a house of prayer. In the temple context prayer was offered three times a day – morning, mid-day, and evening. Remember, Jesus' allusion back to Isaiah – the temple had become a place that was functioning as something of a deterrent to prayer. Fifth, temple prayers were not as broad ranging as prayers tend to be today – we, in my view, make it up as we go along. It was not this way in the Jewish context where prayer was focused on confession, the validity of sacrifice for forgiveness, and serving God with a contrite heart. My wager is that this verse has these limited contexts in mind and therefore is not a *blank check* for whatever the disciples, or us for that matter, ask for. Rather, it is attuned to temple prayer and therefore "in prayer" has a definite context wherein the prayers offered relate to faith in God answering because this is based in his character and intentions that were known when it came to prayer. To ask in this context is to believe that one receives what is asked for.

In verse 25, we see more – such praying has to take place in the specific context of forgiveness, already a condition no doubt for the previous, yet the aim here is to stress a unity of community of forgiveness so that God, in turn, will forgive the prayer's sin. Believing that true forgiveness of someone in the community of disciples took place, not only leads to forgiveness of that disciple's sin, but it is, as it were, an asking in prayer that is then received, and therefore becomes one's own.

In the next scene in the story, we have an extended debate and confrontation with Jesus and the Jerusalem religious elite in the temple area. Now back in Jerusalem and the temple, the previous time sequences drop out. Jesus is then questioned concerning his actions. The religious elite wants to know where his authority comes from, though we may wonder, based on the narrator's remark back in verse 18 about wanting to kill him, just how seriously they really want to know the source of Jesus' authority. Jesus has acted authoritatively in "these things;" meaning what he has done in the temple area, and the crowds are amazed, but the religious elite is highly suspicious – implying that authority needed to come from them and it had not.

The reply of Jesus, as so often, is to ask another question, before answering one posed to him. He raises his query concerning John, who had gained unprecedented popularity with the people: John's baptism, he asks, was it from heaven or human beings? Notice Jesus' double, "Answer me" in verses 24-30 is a way of his taking charge of this confrontation on authority. This bold challenge causes a fair amount of consternation on the part of the religious elite, and they discuss their response. Should they answer from heaven (and here they show their rejection of John), Jesus will ask why they didn't believe his pronouncements concerning the KOG and the Messiah. Should they answer from human beings, they face the belief of the people that John was a prophet and they are afraid. Their answer then is – "We don't know." On the basis of the religious elite's response, Jesus refuses to go any further. His emphatic "I's" here, nevertheless, stress his authority over that of his questioners, while also showing them that they are not in the position they assume is theirs.

The wiles of deception have blinded the religious elite, and they are ill-equipped to deal with the questions and the authority of Jesus. Again, Jesus is portrayed as initiating controversy through subversive actions and teaching – crossing boundaries of well-worn traditions and radically suggesting God is doing something new.

12:1 – 44

Jesus' return to Jerusalem and the temple has resulted in a confrontation with the religious elite over his authority to challenge the present ways the temple was operating. The radical and subversive actions in the temple area will eventually turn out to be one of the key events that contribute to Jesus going to his death. While the previous story of the debate over authority in chapter 11 showed Jesus taking authority, in chapter 12 we now find the discussion continues.

Moving on to tell a parable, Jesus intends to uphold memories of God and Israel, which often was symbolized by a planter and a vineyard. Before looking at this parable a little more carefully, let me give you five reasons Jesus taught in parables:

To capture attention;
to subvert and reveal;
to make people think for themselves;
to pose questions, not give cut and dried answers;
to invoke a response through images and symbols of the stories.

The person who planted this vineyard is heavily invested—vines, walls, wine press, and watchtower would have been a significant financial outlay for the owner. Renting such a property would be a familiar way of doing things in this cultural context and payment, after a few years of waiting for new vines to produce, would give the tenants the time they needed to be able to pay the owner a part of the harvest for the rent.

After sending many servants to the tenants who fail to collect his rent the owner of the vineyard finally sends a son whom he loves. Just as God has repeatedly sent prophets to Israel and they were mistreated and killed, Jesus implies he is the sent son who is loved, and who soon, according to the storyline, will also be killed.

At the end of the parable, it is the owner who finally comes and kills the tenants and turns the vineyard over to others. This may anticipate the future destruction of the temple, which we have already seen has been implied earlier and will be made explicit later in chapter 13, and the vindication of Jesus through his resurrection.

This story precipitates a challenge from Jesus, quoting Psalm 118:23, which metaphorically transfers the imagery from vineyards to stones, perhaps supporting the implication that the parable finds its nexus in the religious elite and the temple. The rejected stone, in fact, becomes the piece that holds everything together, reversing what one would have assumed to be the case. God therefore again brings about new perspectives for those who have ears to hear and eyes to see.

The shocking character of this parabolic recounting incites the religious elite to think about arresting Jesus, yet again the crowd; the lingering crowd in the story still appears sympathetic to Jesus' critiques. This continues to breed fear in the religious elite, and they take no action.

Following the parable and the growing awareness by the religious elite that Jesus means trouble, the chief priests, teachers of the law, and the elders send some Pharisees and Herodians with the aim of catching Jesus in theological or political apostasy. Their strategy seems to be to flatter Jesus, although their false intentions may turn out to be closer to the truth than they may perceive.

The issue they raise is the hotly disputed matter of Roman taxes. These taxes would have been a thorn in the side of the Jews, confirming their ongoing state of exile. Many would have grudgingly paid them, but plotted out and longed for the day when they would be free from such hostile and oppressive political domination.

If Jesus supports paying he may appear pro-Roman – if he suggests not paying, he may be considered a subversive renegade and a threat to Roman authority. Jesus, however, has not been taken in by the subterfuge. Intriguingly, he asks for a denarius to look at. This coin would have had the image of the Roman emperor and an inscription that would have noted his divine status. Image and inscription on those coins amounted to raising widespread anger among Jews, for it reminded them of their political subjection, and even worse, was an offense to their God.

Jesus has no problem looking at the coin in spite of the potential Jewish accusations of treason or idolatry. There is no reason not to pay tax to Caesar – it is permitted, in the sense of giving back to, or reimbursing a debt that is owed – according to Jesus a tax is payable, so it should be paid and doing so is not to be considered a betrayal of God.

Giving to Caesar, the coin with his image and inscription, for tax purposes is not to be considered as necessarily in conflict with giving to God what is God's, which at the outset would be following Jesus. The point here seems to be ownership – no doubt God and Caesar have distinct regions of ownership, but they may also have some that are related. It seems then that Jesus is confirming that it is possible to do both. Paying tax does not mean that one is pro-Roman and therefore anti-God. A distinction, however, though it is not addressed here, might arise if Caesar were to require something that went against God. This configuration of Jesus to do both astonishes all who have heard. He has taken the trap against him and turned it back on those who set it.

The next interlocutors to approach Jesus in the temple area are the Sadducees, who the narrator comments, do not believe in resurrection. They too address Jesus politely and respectfully, yet perhaps with the slight intonation of irony, in order to set Jesus up for a comparison with a real theological heavyweight such as Moses. The Sadducees' complex scenario is connected to the OT (Deuteronomy 25:5-6) view of what is called Levirate law, where a man's life is viewed in continuity with the children he produces. When a man died without a son his widow was to marry his brother – her brother-in-law – and then hope to have a son who could carry on the name of the dead brother. The question, however, in our context, is more pointedly – after all these types of marriages whose wife would the woman be at resurrection?

Jesus' response suggests the Sadducees are deceived, do not know the Scriptures, nor are they acquainted with the power of God. He implies in his next point that whenever (!) dead people rise, something the Sadducees are ignorant of on two accounts - the Scriptures and God's power - there will be no marriage as traditionally understood. This is because God will change people to be like angels, and therefore the problem they raise, albeit focused on a sort of a hoax, turns out to not be a problem for God.

Turning next to address the more general issue of resurrection itself, Jesus appeals to a text the Sadducees would have accepted as authoritative. While it is not immediately clear how Jesus is intending Exodus 3:6 to support resurrection of God's people, he may be creatively highlighting a transfer from past statements to future realities, pointing to the resurrection of Abraham, Isaac, and Jacob even though they died. If this is the case, "I am" here underscores that resurrection is deeply embedded in the character of God. The ongoing capacity to live is not due to a son's carrying on the family name, but to the "I am-ness" of God, who is the God of the living, not the dead. As God is the God of the living, the Sadducees are mistaken in their views about denying resurrection. Jesus returns at the end of this dialogue to remind them they are deceived in this matter.

After the two previous attempts to trap or trip Jesus, the narrator introduces a teacher of the law who has been listening to all of this. He assesses that Jesus has taught well and his answers capably given, yet he has his own question: which commandment is of first importance? Getting a running start, so to speak, Jesus first appeals to Deuteronomy 6:4 to establish the theological framing for his comments about the most important commandment and then to Deuteronomy 6:5 and Leviticus 19:18 to make his case. The linkage between loving God and loving neighbor is so close that Jesus mentions them together. Purposefully, he wants to stress that these commandments are the greatest so that the scribe cannot merely privilege the first one and ignore the second.

The scribe applauds this teaching, a fairly courageous act considering the temple area location and the previous highly suspicious attitudes of the religious elite towards Jesus. In fact, this man goes even further than applause in recognizing the whole sacrificial system should be subsumed to loving God and neighbor. Jesus confirms that this scribe has keen insight into the new perspectives he is bringing and subtly challenges him to draw even closer to the reign of God, something that he is already well on his way toward doing. These responses from Jesus in the temple have brought an end to a flurry of questions for the moment, and in what comes next Jesus will pose a few himself. Still teaching in the temple area, he now takes a moment to raise questions about the Messiah. He wants to know why the scribes refer to the Messiah as the Son of David? He then quotes Psalm 110:1 to show that the Messiah is David's Lord and if David refers to him in this manner he cannot be merely his son, according to human ancestry, which is perhaps accurate, but not an adequate perception of the true Messiah. By this time, Jesus is attracting more widespread attention, and crowds in the temple area are gladly listening to him. As the attentive crowd is listening to his teaching favorably, Jesus turns to critique the hypocrisy of some scribes as they flaunt their position in self-serving actions of exploitation and arrogance. They, Jesus promises, will be judged severely.

The last teaching in the temple area consists of underlining the sacrificial giving of a widow. This shows the disciples that people, not amounts are important to God. Many give out of surplus; she gives out of her lack, which means she sets out or is a picture of a new perspective concerning the importance of the generosity of giving, even if you have little to give.

13:1 – 37

The interpretive background and present understanding of this chapter are not only complex, but somewhat inconclusive. There are differences of exegesis and opinions range from more to less literal readings.

The story continues in verses 1-4. Jesus now, according to the narrator, departs from the temple. An unnamed disciple comments on the size of the edifice and Jesus, while acknowledging this, proposes that nothing of it will left standing.

The next scene shifts to sitting on the Mount of Olives. Jesus is with the first four disciples, who were called at the beginning of the story. Then the question. When will this come about and what will be the sign of all these things being completed? Messiah that he is, Jesus responds in verses 5-37, in a rather enigmatic manner. What comes first is a warning. Beware! There will be many false messiahs who will lead many away from the path to life. Rumors of wars and battles will take place, earthquakes and famines will also arise, but all these are merely the beginning, not the end.

More explicitly now in the story, Jesus rivets his attention on his disciples. Beware! Prepare yourselves! During this period of time of the destruction of the temple, you who follow me are going to face severe Jewish and Roman persecution because you are my disciples and will be my testimony. Seemingly somewhat 'forced' in between verse 9 and 11, Jesus declares in verse 10 that these difficulties will take place within the context of the "good news" *first* (more to come) being proclaimed to Gentiles. Meanwhile, verse 11 looks back at the probable trial scene of verse 10; the disciples can rest assured that the Spirit will speak for them in the midst of this most frightening undertaking. As if all this weren't bad enough for the disciples, familial relations will become suspect and terrifying, resulting in hatred and even death for those who dare to align themselves with Jesus, but those who persevere to the end (somewhat ambiguous as to when that is) will be saved.

Then the rising threat to the temple and the people in Judea increases to the point of no return in verses 14-23. When this somewhat puzzling desolation for us (though readers then should recognize it), echoing the story of Daniel occurs, it's time to flee. No matter what your circumstances or where you are, the warning is to get out immediately. This will be more complicated for some than others, so pray that the departure will not be in winter. Suffering will be immense, as represented through Jesus' words offered to readers by the narrator. His comparative pronouncement here in verse 19, not to be taken literally, was likely to have been sort of standard usage for monumental and horrific circumstances of awful distress. Had God not come to the rescue, even the elect would have been lost, so God cuts these days short for their sake. As previously, in verses 5-6, Jesus then announces there will be many charlatans who make messianic and prophetic claims only to lead astray. They are false. Disciples are to be alert! Stay the course.

Some interpreters suggest that the next part of the story moves from the fall of the temple and Jerusalem to the end of the world. What follows in verses 24-31, however, actually gets closer to answering part of the original question posed by the disciples back in verse 4, so it seems better to understand these sayings as still dealing with the coming destruction of the center of Jewish life; Jerusalem and its temple. Same subject, same scenario. Linking into to a long line of prophetic succession (Isaiah 13:10; Ezekiel 32:7) in verses 24-25, what does dramatically shift at this moment is a new and striking use of metaphorical language depicting the natural world. But what's the point? Jesus, in using this prophetic repertoire, targets these pictures at Jerusalem as representing its destruction. Something new is going to happen here. Building off this symbolic clout, Jesus, in his familiar *Son of Man* self-reference, connects himself with the Daniel 7:13-14 figure that comes to the Ancient of Days to receive power and authority to reign over the world. The Son of Man, in the resurrected life, will replace and go beyond the temple and all it stood for by bringing the received power and authority to bear first of all in judging Israel and its holy city and sacred place and by sending out angels to gather (in the OT Jewish captives) – or now bring together the elect from the whole world; creating a *new people* of God.

And then, at last, in verses 28-29 Jesus responds to the question of the disciples about *when* and a *sign*. He offers them a metaphorical picture; a way to discern when the temple will fall. Thus, Jesus, as it were, *signs in* with the reference to the fig tree (remember 11:12-21). Like the time when it becomes ready to bear fruit, the disciples will know that what they are *seeing* ("these things" referring to verses 14-22f) leading up to the destruction of the temple, now means the time is at hand. The impending has now arrived. That *time* is even more definitively marked out in verse 30; "Amen, I say to you" the ruin predicted will take place during your generation. To underline the force of the previous *time* factor, Jesus authoritative proclamation in verse 31 points out that his word is sustainable and rock solid (like God's word in the OT; Isaiah 40), even more so than heaven and earth, which were about the closest things, in this context, that would be unlikely to disappear. Hence, through all that's going to happen in the lifetime of the disciples they can trust the words of Jesus concerning his predictions of the disastrous events that were soon to take place in Jerusalem.

The last part of this chapter from verse 32 announces a change of subject; moving from the when and sign of the fall of Jerusalem to the when of the final return of Jesus, or from the *known* to the *unknown*. Intriguingly, Jesus has given the disciples a *sign* and a *time* for the woes of Israel. They know *when* this will happen; it will precede his end time re-coming to earth and take place in their own age – but Jesus clearly wants to distinguish this information from the *when* of the end – which no one knows, except the father. Thus, the two timings are not to be assimilated *as if* the fall of the temple would be the end of the world.

While Jesus has previously warned his followers about being misled by charlatans on the ground pretending to be Messiahs, he now stresses the need to pay close attention to his own true Messianic post-resurrection return to earth, which may take place anytime as illustrated by the little story in verses 34-36. Stay alert! Be ready here applies not merely to the four disciples on the Mount of Olives, but to all.

14:1 – 72

The narrator returns, back in a more direct voice, and next recounts the prelude to the destiny of Jesus. Setting the scene for the unfolding story of the Passover and the festival of Unleavened Bread allows the narrator to again bring in the covert plans of the enemies of Jesus, who want to see him dead. That is, while these Jewish ceremonies are at hand, and hundreds are on their way to Jerusalem to celebrate, there are some who are already planning a devious act to remove Jesus once and for all. Yet, the narrator wants readers to know that these adversaries of Jesus do not want to risk stirring the crowds up, who already it seems are somewhat supportive of Jesus. After privileging the reader with this information, the scenario shifts to Bethany.

This anointing story, while a lovely act of honor, still enhances the foreboding sense of death that hangs over Jesus. An unnamed woman enters the house and pours an expensive oil/perfume over his head. Some unnamed disciples find this to be a waste and allege that it would have been better used for the poor. Exceptionally, because this is *death time*, the unnamed woman has indeed performed an action that Jesus not only accepts, but praises. The poor, as important as they are, will surely be able to be served after Jesus' death, while the moment he, the guests, disciples, and the woman are now in is unique and unrepeatable. Thus, she is to be left alone. Jesus interprets her act as an anointing his body for burial, which in his eyes is both fitting and good. In fact, this act is so important ("Amen, I say to you"), not only as a prelude to Jesus' death, but Jesus goes remarkably beyond this by far. He alludes to the gospel being proclaimed in the whole world, and as it is the act of this anonymous woman, as Jesus understands it, that will be recalled in *memory* of her. Thus, in a quite stunning fashion at this pre-death stage, Jesus, through the narrator, announces that his impending death will come to be viewed as *part of the good news*. Death will not be the end of his story.

Then, the narrator once again takes readers, as it were, to the sidelines. They are reminded that in spite of earlier crowd concerns, the enemies of Jesus are still interested in doing away with him and thus are pleased to meet Judas and to accept his offer to betray him.

Returning from this short, but essential detour, we find the disciples asking Jesus about preparations for *him* to eat a Passover meal. Jesus, likely to have already made plans, sends two disciples with instructions on what to say and do, which the narrator confirms works out precisely as planned. All has been made ready.

Once the meal begins, as tradition calls for *in the evening*, Jesus makes a striking "Amen, I say to you" announcement that someone at the meal festivities will be his betrayer. Following this surprising assertion each disciple wants to know who it's going to be – "is it I?" Jesus will only reveal that it is one of the Twelve at the meal. Whoever it is (we readers already know), Jesus says it would be better if this one had not been born.

In verses 22-25, the scene now more directly opens onto *meal time*. Jesus takes a monumental moment to inaugurate the symbolic gesture concerning the repertoire *bread and wine*, representing his eventual dead body and blood, as a sacrifice in the making of a (new) covenant (Exodus 24:8) to be participated in by all the disciples and many others after them. Then, another "Amen, I say to you" in verse 25 strikes at the heart of the matter: the death of Jesus, yet notice this is not the end of the story since this saying looks forward to his *re-drinking* wine at some undetermined point post-death.

After singing, perhaps some version or parts of Psalms 113-115, Jesus and the disciples leave *meal time* to return to the *Mount of Olives time*, which presents the occasion for another revelation of shock and consternation. Jesus tells his disciples: they all will desert him. To enlarge the horizon of this disquieting announcement, Zechariah 13 is *sighted* with the narrator adding a mysterious 'I' to the equation. When the shepherd is executed, the sheep will scatter. That much is clear. But this is quickly turned in another direction. Jesus proclaims that he will be raised (already predicted several times in the story 8:31; 9:31), and then gather his sheep (disciples) going before them into home territory; Galilee. Abruptly, but with no reference to the 'raising,' Peter immediately denies that he will desert Jesus. Yet Jesus does not share his affirmation of loyalty and strongly asserts "Amen, I say to you" that Peter will soon deny him three times before the cock crows twice. And then quite brashly, Peter refuses to accept this premonition and expresses solidarity to even die with Jesus, which all the other disciples equally affirm for themselves.

The narrator now shifts scenes to focus on the complexities of Gethsemane and betrayal, and will only pick up the previous denial thread later in the story. Jesus instructs his disciples to wait as he goes to pray, though he does take Peter, James, and John along with him further, perhaps since they are, at least on the story level, present at other exceptional occasions (5.37; 9:2). He is disturbed and stressed by the impending event of his death and the reality of it drawing closer and closer to actuality. Moving on even further now, but alone, Jesus goes to the ground and prays that he might not have to experience *death time* and if possible avoid it all together. Subsequently, he then prays more directly and shockingly to Abba, an intimate Aramaic term for Father, an address that seems to be exceptionally used by him in this special way. Acknowledging the possibilities of his Father, Jesus again put the matter of imminent suffering and death, symbolized by *this cup*, before God and asks that it be taken away, yet Jesus is willing to follow the directions of his Father, wherever they may lead. Returning to the three disciples, who have been instructed to wait and keep their eyes open, Jesus finds them asleep, not once, but each of the three times he returns from praying. The weakness of those who, a few moments ago in the story, claimed to be stalwart supporters of Jesus is all too evident. They're having serious trouble staying awake, even in the midst of this *dramatic* moment. Jesus takes little time waiting for a prayer response, while also now rousing his drowsy disciples – Enough! – the Son of Man is now going to be betrayed, so let's go and get on with it.

The Markan narrator concurs and emphasizes that this betrayal sequence takes place "immediately," even as Jesus was still speaking to the three. And so it is, a kiss from Judas betrays Jesus, perhaps a necessary 'sign' in the darkness and an armed mob from the chief priests, scribes, and elders begin to lead him away. As the temple mobsters grab Jesus, the narrator recounts, seemingly without a high degree of relevance for the story, that someone cuts off the ear of, perhaps the leader (the slave of the high priest) of these *official* thugs. What, however, is more important is this mob-like violence scenario, Jesus suggests, is all a bit ridiculous since he is not a villain and they should recognize this as he had previously and on many occasions taught in the temple where they could have taken him at any time. Jesus will not resist and is ready for his death and for the scriptures to be fulfilled. Just then, he is deserted – abandoned by those who had fervently promised not to do so.

Following this, in verses 51-52, for some reason perhaps only really known to the narrator, there is a rather bizarre recounting of a young man dressed in a linen cloth who followed Jesus. He seems to have been identified as such by the mob, at least to the degree that it attempts to grab him, but to no avail as he slips, perhaps as it were, out of the grasp of those *holding* onto the cloth, and dashes away naked.

The next sequence of the narrative moves readers directly into a new and uncomfortable environment. Jesus is brought before the high priest; the chief priests, scribes, and elders for questioning, though the minds of the previously mentioned, we're likely to have already been made up. The story again momentarily goes behind the main scene to remind the reader that Peter is still, yet at a *distance*, somewhat in the picture. Meanwhile, the omniscient narrator recounts that Jesus' enemies are attempting to establish some valid indictments against him in order to put him to death, but to no avail. False testimonies abound, and no agreement between them was to be found. Jesus could have been declared innocent, but such a dubious and deceptive gathering will go to any lengths to see him condemned.

This very direction is presently employed by the high priest who takes over the process and explicitly questions Jesus, aiming to draw a response where one is far from warranted in light of the fiasco of the incongruent testimonies. He is rightly silent. But then a further query comes from the high priest. "Are you the Messiah (Christ), the son of the Blessed" (avoiding the use of the name God)? Jesus categorically responds, "I am" and the story explodes in Christological significance. Indeed, this is a startling and an extraordinary self-acknowledgment in the narrative context where the greater stress on the non-revealing (8:27-30) of his identity has been paramount until now. In contrast to that which has preceded, this is *revelation time*. But, as remarkable as this is, it is not all. Jesus continues and in so doing clarifies his vision of the Messiah, which was no doubt very different from the council and its leaders. "And you will *see* the Son of Man sitting at the right hand of the Power (avoiding the use of the name God) and coming with the clouds of heaven." Interweaving Daniel 7:13 and Psalm 110:1 in a metaphorical manner, Jesus announces that whatever the outcome of this charade being put on by the high priest and the others, the Son of Man will be vindicated, likely through resurrection, the reception of a *place* with God, and the impending fall of Jerusalem and its most sacred *place*.

At this stage of the story, the high priest tears his clothes and poses a rhetorical question concerning why any witnesses are necessary. Of course, that possibility had already failed them, so the logical conclusion is; none are needed at this point. Then the reason: Jesus is accused of blasphemy and all present have heard his words. This charge may have been based on a number of possibilities: his manner of speaking of himself, which could have been interpreted as arrogance towards God; his reference to sitting at God's right hand; his refusal to acknowledge the leaders of God's people, yet the Markan narrator passes over this without giving any explanation for the indictment. The high priest then poses a final rhetorical question to the group: "How does it appear to you?" The response: Condemnation deserving death. Such a verdict causes some to abuse Jesus in various sorts of ways, including blindfolding and beating him and then challenging him to prophesy, perhaps concerning who struck him.

Meanwhile, as the narrator now reminds readers (14:54), Peter who followed Jesus at a distance post-betrayal, has been nearby warming himself by the fire. A servant passing by sees him and perhaps looking inquisitively at him suggests that he was with Jesus of Nazareth. This identification results in three denials by Peter. First, he neither knows nor understands what the servant has said. After this, he changes location and moves away into the forecourt and then the cock crows. The servant, seemingly coming along, mentions to others in the forecourt that Peter is one who was with Jesus. Second, he denies this. Then the bystanders who heard the servant reaffirm that surely Peter is one of the followers of Jesus since he is a Galilean. Third, he strongly by oath denies that he even knows the person of whom they are speaking. "Immediately," so often used by the narrator of the story to reinforce *at once time*, the cock crows, fulfilling the prediction Jesus made back at the Mount of Olives. Peter recalls Jesus' words (14:30) and weeps.

15:1 – 47

"Immediately" in the early hours (first light) connects this sequence to the previous night as the story rushes on to its denouement. The narrator informs readers, the whole Jewish council, which has no authority to put Jesus to death, meets to finalize its strategy of accusation. Jesus is bound and brought to Pilate, who the council well knows does have the power, in representing Rome, to execute him. The narrator, wasting no time with formalities, reports that Pilate wants to know if Jesus is the king of the Jews, likely here a question that was one of the strategic ploys of the Jewish leaders to persuade Pilate that Jesus was a political threat to Roman authority. Jesus responds to Pilate with something like: you say so, or well, yes, but this may not be what you assume. The chief priests, now representing the Jewish leadership, feed Pilate more accusations. Intriguingly, there is no follow up with a further question to Jesus about kingship, but Pilate alludes to the numerous charges that are being brought against him, to which Jesus does not respond; no reply.

At *feast time*, Pilate would release a prisoner, according to the wishes of the people. Someone named Barabbas was in prison with rebels who had committed murder. Then the crowd emerges, seemingly sufficiently aware that it was on this day and time that Pilate, as was his custom, would be offering amnesty to an inmate. It requests that he follow through. He responds, who do they want? Pilate proposes to release the "king of the Jews." The omniscience of the narrator now more forcefully comes into play by informing readers that Pilate recognized that it was because of jealously that the chief priests had turned him over. Pilate has seen through their trumped up indictments and cunning maneuvers to *frame* Jesus. But what could he do in light of the persuasive and malicious tactics of the chief priests who provoke the crowd to appeal for the release of Barabbas? Pilate again addresses the crowd. He wants to know what the people suggest he do with the "king of the Jews." They shout, "Crucify him." Pilate asks another question, implying the innocence of Jesus, but no answer is forthcoming and the shouting "Crucify him" remains dominant and decisive. Thus, Pilate in order to satisfy the crowd releases Barabbas, flogs Jesus and hands him over to be crucified.

Roman soldiers further beat and mock him, dressing him in a purple cloak and a crown of thorns, proclaiming "hail, king of the Jews." Little did they know how many dimensions of truth there was in their ironic jesting. Then Jesus, back in his own, at this stage, no doubt rags, is taken off to be crucified.

Simon, probably known to the Markan narrator and his audience, happens to pass by and is enlisted to carry the cross out to Golgotha. In the midst of this, Jesus is offered wine mixed with myrrh, though it's not entirely clear by whom or whether this was for good or ill, but he refuses the drink. Keeping with tradition, as was common in these cases, the soldiers now cast lots for his garments, though one wonders how much of anything of them would be left at this stage of the dire proceedings.

Then......, Jesus is crucified at nine in the morning.

According to Roman custom, there was a notice of some sort attached to the prisoner identifying the crime committed. In Jesus' case, it is "king of the Jews." This *sign* for all to see was intended to convey the message that Jesus was viewed as a traitor and thus judged deserving of death, which would be the horrible end of anyone who cherished such kingly pretentions in the face of Roman authority. To defy Rome in this manner leads to: crucifixion.

Jesus is crucified with two *bandits*, possibly here a reference to zealots; one on the right, the other on the left. The Markan narrator provides no information on these two, which leaves the reader open to a possible recollection: 'right' and 'left' may refer back to where James and John ask to be in this very location with Jesus in his *glory* (10:37). Ironically, neither is now present nor is Jesus anywhere near being glorified (notice that verse 28 is missing in many translations due to it being recognized as a later addition of Isaiah 53:12). Others passing by attest to Jesus' woeful state (this perhaps provoking in the reflections of the narrator a memory of the language of Psalm 22); they shake their heads and taunt him: "So, you're the one who would destroy the temple and rebuild it in three days – Huh! Come on down from that cross and save yourself." This sort of mockery is added to by the chief priests and scribes who gibe – "he saved others but cannot save himself – the Messiah (Christ) — the king of Israel," now the mocking taking on perhaps a more nationalistic tone, "ought to come down from the cross so we can *see* and believe." The narrator adds for completeness that even the two crucified to the right and left of Jesus sneered at him. They too join the cast of scoffers. In the last several hours Jesus has been betrayed, abandoned, and subjected to much abuse and scorn, culminating in the momentous event of the crucifixion.

This is further actualized by the narrator who recounts the darkness at noon, which covers the region (land) and lasts until three in the afternoon, perhaps representing a sign of God's judgment. It is at this point that Jesus shouts out a rendering of Psalm 22:1 in Aramaic, translated into Greek by the narrator, and into English as: "My God, my God, why have you forsaken me?" Jesus senses a deep alienation from God, and this expression underscores his awareness of being actively abandoned in the midst of his agonizing death. Some at the cross assume he is calling Elijah. A person runs off to soak a sponge with inexpensive wine (vinegar) to give Jesus a drink and for some reason reinforces the previous reference to Elijah and suggests waiting and *seeing* if he will rescue him. Jesus then cries out and 'expires' – breathes his last. And the temple curtain is torn from top to bottom (some approximately 25 meters), representing that God, instead of entirely forsaking Jesus, actually with this divine act begins vindicating him as the new place and space for his people, as the old temple is prefigured to now be on its way towards destruction. After this, in contrast to those who ridiculed Jesus, a centurion who directly observes his death, proclaims with remarkable Christological insight, "Truly, this man was (a) (the) Son of God."

Intriguingly, because the focus has previously been on male disciples, the narrator mentions women near the scene of the cross, observing the crucifixion of Jesus from a distance. These three women, Mary Magdalene, Mary the mother of James the younger and Joses, and Salome were *followers* of Jesus and part his work in Galilee. They are likely mentioned here by name since they had a closer contact with Jesus than a larger, perhaps less involved, group of women who also came with him from Galilee to Jerusalem. While the men have abandoned Jesus, these women are portrayed as faithful followers and witnesses to his terrifying end.

At around sunset, Joseph of Arimathea, described as a prominent leader of the Jews and as one looking for the Kingdom of God, goes *boldly* before Pilate to request Jesus' dead body before the Sabbath. According to Jewish Sabbath codes nothing as adventurous as a burial could be permitted that day, so Joseph needed to act quickly if he was to preserve the law and likely pay respect to Jesus. Once Pilate astonished that Jesus could already be dead (a death like this might take much longer), and thus needing a confirmation from the centurion, finds out that indeed Jesus has died, he allows Joseph to take the dead body. No small task and in a hurry Joseph, likely with help, purchases a linen cloth and takes the body down from the cross. He wraps the dead body in the cloth and places it in a tomb made out of rock and then seals it with a stone. Intriguingly, the narrator recounts that two of the three women that were present near the cross scene, Mary Magdalene and Mary the mother of Joses, see where the body was laid. This opens the way for the day after the Sabbath.

16:1 - 8

The two Mary's and Salome had bought spices to anoint Jesus, perhaps not previously having had time for this in a rush to get Jesus' dead body buried before Sabbath. At around sunrise, they go to the tomb. They were concerned about who would move the large stone that sealed the tomb to enable them to enter and discussed this among themselves. Yet, when they arrive the stone is no longer there; so they go into the tomb, see a young man dressed in a white robe, and are frightfully astonished. This controversial character in the story, it appears, is not any normal young man. His white robe may be translucent, likely denoting an angel, and thus accounting for the strong reaction of the women. The messenger of God then tells the women not to fear, confirms they are looking for Jesus of Nazareth, who was crucified and announces, "He has been raised. He is not here. Behold where they put him. But go tell his disciples and Peter that he is going before you to Galilee; there you will see (reconnect with) him as he told you." On the narrative level, the words of the young man are fascinating and strongly resonate with the previous resurrection sayings of Jesus. And then the women flee, perplexed and trembling, and say nothing to anyone, for they were afraid. What an utterly astounding ending to this most remarkable story. Whether the narrator intended to finish the narrative here at 16:8 is a hotly disputed issue. Since many major commentaries cover the interpretive options, it is not necessary to discuss them here. My wager is that in spite of the understandable, but wayward response of the women, the affirmation, especially at 14:28, the words of God's emissary here at 16:6-7, and the coalescence with the overarching narrative arc, give plenty of credence to the story of Jesus resurrection. Surely, the disciples would have returned to Galilee crushed, but with at least a fleeting memory of Jesus telling them he would be raised and go before them *post-death time* to Galilee. When we consider that this gospel story exists at all and that in fact there are several others written in a somewhat similar vein, it appears that something happened to give rise to such accounts. Thus, it is likely that *resurrection time* is a reality for Jesus in Jerusalem, and then for his disciples when they see him in Galilee, as it is for the many who follow in the footsteps of Jesus from those days until "that day" (13:32), unknown to anyone, except God.

www.ingramcontent.com/pod-product-compliance
Lightning Source LLC
Chambersburg PA
CBHW021443080526
44588CB00009B/661